PADDLING
&NORTHWEST MONTANA
GLACIER NATIONAL PARK

40 Paddling Locations

Written & Illustrated By: ***Debra J. Arnold***

Front cover picture of Flathead Lake, Northwestern Montana, courtesy of Jon Maxwell

ISBN 978-1-5323-0980-9

PREFACE

This paddling guide encompasses 40 of the finest paddling locations in Northwestern Montana and Glacier National Park. This part of the Northwest is a hidden gem for paddling, and possibly the most wild and scenic inland area to paddle in the lower 48. It's also one of the few places left where you can find the full compliment of wildlife for forested and mountainous areas, including apex predators like wolves and grizzly bears.

The book also provides information on safety, boats (personal watercraft), and equipment that will help make paddling experiences safe and enjoyable. The scope of this book, however, is limited to basic information on these topics as the main focus is "where to paddle."

The paddling sites described here are favorites of the author and her paddling buddies in the Flathead Paddlers group, a non-profit organization dedicated to the enjoyment and enhancement of knowledge and skills related to paddling. If you're interested in learning more about this organization, finding paddling partners, and/or joining, please check out the club's website at: groups/yahoo.com/group/flatheadpaddlers/. Questions, comments, and notations of any errors in this edition can be directed to the author, Debra Arnold, at: ladyckayaker@yahoo.com.

TABLE OF CONTENTS

A SHIP IS SAFE IN HARBOR,
BUT THAT IS NOT WHAT
SHIPS ARE BUILT FOR.
~John A. Shedd~

LAKE McDONALD, GLACIER NATIONAL PARK

INTRODUCTION

Grab a paddle! It's your ticket to get up close and personal with the great outdoors. It allows you a chance to slow down and de-stress, to genuinely be "in the moment" as your paddle glides smoothly through the water and propels you to new adventures. Paddling allows you to experience wilderness, wildlife, spectacular scenery, and a chance to build lasting memories of good times with paddling buddies. Or, you can recharge your spirit with solitude and the rhythmic movements of your paddle strokes. (And, yes, you'll need something to paddle as well)!

All this and more are available in abundance in Northwestern Montana, a premier paddling destination with both Glacier National Park and Flathead Lake within its boundaries. Glacier Park is appropriately called the "gem of the continent", and Flathead Lake is the largest fresh water lake west of the Mississippi. Water here is clear and pure. What a concept! Its color ranges from deep blues and aquamarines to emerald green in the shallows. Spring run-off can make the rivers and lake inflows murky, but you can generally see 30-40 ft. below your boat/board quite easily.

In addition to clear water, the snow-capped and cathedral-like spires of numerous mountain ranges provide a backdrop for scenic beauty that's a clear "10" on most peoples' scales. Add the incredible variety of birds and wildlife, including grizzly and black bears, moose, elk, and bighorn sheep, and you have a recipe for paddling heaven – probably the best inland place to paddle in the entire country!

Scope of book

This book covers 40 destinations in northwest Montana that are only a sampling of the many possibilities for paddling in this wild country liberally interspersed with glacial "potholes". The sites described here are mostly "flat water" (lakes, sloughs, ponds). Also included are a few water trails that are (seasonally) slow, meandering rivers that empty into lakes (inflows). Faster, whitewater, rivers are a whole different ballgame and are outside the scope of this book.

Book Format, Maps

The 40 paddling destinations are arranged into geographical sections. All locations are described in terms of time and mileage from Kalispell, MT which is located slightly off center of the Flathead Valley north of Flathead Lake. And, the sequence of destinations in each section extends from the closest to the furthest.

Paddle craft recommendations (or, sometimes, non-recommendations) are made for each site along with the paddler's suggested skill level. These suggestions match anticipated paddling distance and common wind/wave conditions encountered. Keep in mind, however, that wind and waves come up quickly on mountain lakes, and a paddling site rated "beginner" may soon change to intermediate or advanced depending on conditions.

Skill Rating Characteristics:

- **Beginner:** "Never Ever" to tentative paddle strokes, some instability in boat, low level boat/board maneuverability, and ability to paddle only a mile or less on flat water
- **Advanced beginner:** Ability to: easily maneuver boat/board, be relaxed and stable in a boat, paddle 2-5 miles, brace, perform wet exits and re-entry into paddling craft, be comfortable paddling in light wind/waves
- **Intermediate:** Mastery of several paddle strokes, ability to: paddle efficiently and comfortably, easily maneuver boat/board, brace effectively, paddle into winds of 10 mph and 1.5 ft. waves, easily get back into/onto boat/board
- **Advanced:** Ability to: roll (kayaks), perform advanced re-entry skills and paddling strokes, brace instinctively, paddle in winds up to 15 mph and waves up to 2 ft., paddle 20 miles or more/day

Outing distances and approximate times are given for each paddling site, along with directions to the launch area(s). Special interest items are noted that make the particular paddle unique, such as shoreline petroglyphs or kayak camping possibilities. Cautions are given for the particular site such as water flow (enough, or too little). The "Paddle Notes" describe a particular paddle route that was chosen for maximizing the areas of interest and minimizing boat traffic. The represented route by no means represents all possibilities in a given location.

Maps for this booklet have been loosely hand drawn and simplified from several sources including "Google Maps" and a variety of printed Montana maps. Two common symbols used are the "little kayak guy" for the launch, and a teepee for a camping area. On some of the maps, inflows and outflows are noted. All of the Glacier National Park maps depict hiking trails as dotted lines, and several of the maps from other sites do as well.

MANY GLACIER AREA OF GLACIER NATIONAL PARK

SAFETY

Water Safety, Wind & Waves

Northwest Montana and Glacier National Park receive more than a million visitors annually. Many of those folks don't realize that Mother Nature's water safety rules are a bit different here. Aside from the cold water (even in summer), wind picks up very quickly on high mountain lakes, often in less than 5 minutes! And, if you're out in the middle of even a small to medium-sized lake, getting to shore before hypothermia sets in can be a significant problem. Check weather forecasts before you go out, and keep checking often if you're out all day or overnight.

Many of the lakes described here, especially those in Glacier Park, are significantly longer than their width. This causes a long "fetch" which means a lengthy area where the waves can build up from one end to the other. Additionally, wave energy builds around points, corners, or "pinch-points" (where the shoreline pinches together). Sometimes, waves are double in height and intensity in these areas, so it's important to consider the shoreline topography as you paddle.

Wind generally comes up around mid-day or in the afternoons as hotter air rises and creates wind, often from the south, west, or southwest. In mountainous terrain, katabatic winds occur when colder air moves down from the surrounding mountains. Thunderstorms and squalls are always a possibility on mountain lakes, especially during the summer. Remember to get off the water immediately if there's any chance of lightning.

If there are islands or bays where you're paddling and the wind comes up quickly, sometimes you can take shelter in the "lee" of the island. This is the shoreline (in the case of an island) that's opposite from the direction the wind is coming from. If there are trees or the island is elevated, it will provide you shelter. Bays, especially is they have high side cliffs may offer similar protection.

Hypothermia & PFD's

High mountain lakes are cold. Period! Even if the surface temperature feels slightly warm, 5-10 inches under the surface the temperature can be as much as 15-20 degrees colder. And, remember, if you end up "swimming", most of your body is going to be in that colder water. Depending on the water temperature and your body mass (the less body mass, the quicker you get cold), hypothermia can hit you in as little as 5 minutes.

As your body cools, hypothermia renders your hands less dexterous, so it's more difficult to do important things with them – like get back in your boat or on your board! But, the most important thing that cold water steals from you is your brain (i.e., your ability to think clearly)! Cold water shocks your body and makes your brain feel like mush, and everything goes into slow motion. Even things you've practiced many times get 3-5 times more difficult. And, you can't get into a PFD (personal flotation device, or life jacket) in cold water!

1

One of the best ways to keep from drowning in cold water is to wear a PFD securely zipped and snugged around your body. PFD's are required by the U.S. Coast Guard and most states for all personal watercraft. And, they're simply expensive deck ornaments if they're on your boat, not YOU! If your PFD is loose around your body, when you end up in the drink, it'll slip right up to your nose or over your head with your arms flailing. Not a fun position for getting back into a boat or onto a board!

The Canadian Coast Guard tried an experiment a number of years ago with PFD's and cold water in a controlled situation. Several young, strong Coast Guard men, fully dressed, jumped into a pool of water at 40 degrees and were immediately thrown a PFD. Their job was to put the PFD on, zip and snug it and get to the side of the pool. Not one of them could do it, and all would have drowned if they hadn't been pulled out of the water. (reference film could not be found)

So, even on warm days, always wear your PFD. And, how do you wear it? Yep, zipped and snugged! And, make sure you have a PFD made specifically for paddling, as some aren't designed for full arm motion and have a foam collar that gets in the way. You should have free range of motion for your arms in all directions with no chafing. Make sure your PFD fits and is comfortable.

Consider wearing thermal protection when you know the water's cold in spring to early summer or late fall, or when you're paddling a considerable distance in an isolated area. Thermal protection is commonly a wetsuit, or "Farmer John/Jane", a neoprene one piece suit, or it could be a top and bottom. When wet, the close-fitting neoprene insulates your body. A drysuit is another option, although more costly. It keeps you totally dry because of waterproof material and water-tight rubber gaskets at your neck and wrists.

Remember also that you don't have to be in the water to get hypothermia. If you don't bring enough warm clothing, or you've been sweating and the wind comes up, your body can cool quickly. Often, hypothermia isn't recognized because the brain slows down. It's important to get a hypothermic person's core temperature warmed up as quickly as possible, so know what to do (check out the first aid recommendations which are beyond the scope of this book).

Other Safety Recommendations & Environmental Concerns

1. Take a class, or several classes to determine the type of equipment you need and to develop and improve your paddling skills. With education, you will come to have better judgment and a healthier respect for your own abilities, those of others, and inherent risks in different paddling environments.
2. Buy appropriate equipment for the type of paddling you are doing. As an example, if you're planning to paddle 5-10 miles or more with possible wind and waves, a sea kayak with a skirt to keep the water out makes more sense than a small recreational boat or canoe.

3.   Paddle with others if possible, and let someone know your paddling plan. Be sure to check in with them when you return.

4.   When paddling with a group, stay together and paddle at the speed of the slowest paddler. If the group is large enough, you might be able to split into two separate groups regarding paddling speed. Don't leave novices unattended!

5.   Plan your trip destinations (especially open water and longer, overnight trips) carefully and make sure you are properly equipped with survival items such as a first aid kit, survival kit, compass, and maps.

6.   Be flexible and willing to modify your agenda. Sometimes waiting out a storm or high waves simply means delaying a return trip by a few hours, or even a day or two. Often afternoon storms pass by quickly and water calms by early evening. Paddling fatalities have occurred because people felt the need to "stick to the agenda".

7.   Respect wildlife, especially bears in the backcountry and maintain safe distances. Carry bear spray and keep it handy when you land. Prepare and store food and garbage appropriately so animals aren't attracted to campsites. When camping in the backcountry, cook and sleep in separate areas and suspend your food or keep it in closed hatches or backcountry steel food containers (if provided).

8.   Be aware of aquatic invasive species such as milfoil and certain snails that can hitchhike on your boat or board and cause a devastating infestation that can clog and destroy waterways. Inspect your watercraft before you paddle, especially in sensitive areas.

9.   Leave lunch spots and campsites as pristine as you found them.

10. Understand that "you don't know what you don't know". This sounds nonsensical, but your understanding is largely based on your experiences, and it's really hard to comprehend what you haven't experienced. That's why "newbies" can more easily get into trouble on the water because they "don't have a clue".

11. Don't overestimate your abilities/equipment or underestimate conditions.

12. Remember, the most important decision you will make in paddling is the DECISION TO LAUNCH!

BOATS, BOARDS, & GEAR

Boats – It's a good idea to figure out what kind of paddling you want to do before you buy a boat. Do you want to:
- Paddle only close to shore on sunny days with glassy water?
- Paddle for exercise?
- Use your boat like a backpack for backcountry camping?
- Be able to do open water crossings, such as paddling to Wild Horse Island?
- Paddle with friends? (i.e. what kind of boats do they have?)

These are just a few questions to ask yourself, because there are so many different boat designs (for personal watercraft) out there. And, if you choose a boat that isn't designed for the purpose you have in mind, you'll probably be disappointed. More importantly, you could put yourself in danger if you use the boat in conditions for which it's not designed. **You should also consider whether or not your boat will sink (either fully or partially) if you capsize, and if you are able to get back into the boat once you're in the water.** You probably don't think you will ever capsize, but it does happen! It's helpful, therefore, to learn about the different classifications of boats and their characteristics:

TYPES OF KAYAKS

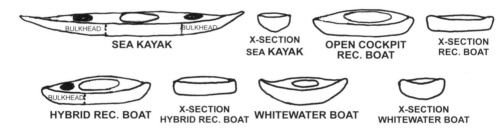

Sea Kayaks – These boats are the "long, skinny" kayaks that are generally 15-18' in length (although some may be as short as 13'). These boats are designed for paddling longer distances, take the least amount of effort to paddle, go faster, and can carry gear for backcountry camping. <u>All sea kayaks have two bulkheads</u> on either side of the cockpit that, with a hatch cover, make two water-tight compartments. The main purpose of the two compartments is flotation, but they can also carry your lunch, jackets, etc. Many sea kayaks can carry two backpack's worth of gear. These boats may be plastic, wood, "skin on frame", or composite (a cloth and resin lay-up such as fiberglass or Kevlar).

When a sea kayak capsizes, the boat floats and water only fills the cockpit. It can easily be turned back over and re-entered (with practice and a paddle float or help from buddies). Spray skirts are generally worn to keep the waves out of the boat, so they are safer to paddle in wind and waves.

4

These boats may feel slightly "tippy" when you're sitting in them and not moving. But, like a bicycle, once they're moving, they're actually more stable than a flat bottom boat. This is because waves go right under the rounder, shallow "V" hulls that don't provide a surface for the waves to push over. On the downside, pricing is generally higher than other boats, and they require a roof rack carrier or boat trailer.

Recreational Kayaks – Recreational kayaks, often called "rec. boats" are brightly colored plastic boats that many box stores carry, and they come in a variety of shapes and sizes. They can be a lot of fun and get you out on the water cheaply and easily (just throw them in the back of a pick-up). But, be careful to use them appropriately. They're designed for leisurely paddling close to shore on flat water, perhaps taking your dog, and having fun on sunny, calm days. Most share the following characteristics:
- They are short (usually less than 10')
- They have a large, open cockpit
- They have a relatively flat, wide bottom

Rec. boats may be open from the bow (front) to the stern (back), or have some foam for partial flotation. These boats feel incredibly stable (not "tippy") when the water's flat, but remember that Mother Nature doesn't always keep the water flat! In wind and waves, rec. boats are the first to capsize when waves catch and flip the wide flat bottoms. When an open cockpit rec. boat capsizes, it can sink, or float upside down a few inches under the water. Water is extremely heavy, and with most designs, you can't tip them back upright or get back in.

Think of the analogy of a tricycle and a bicycle on a flat surface versus a hill. The tricycle tips over easily on a hillside, just like a rec. boat does in medium-sized waves. As previously mentioned, sea kayaks act more like bicycles on a hill when in waves.

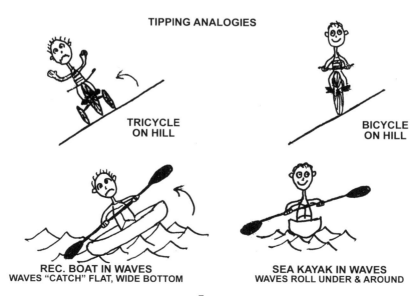

TIPPING ANALOGIES

TRICYCLE ON HILL

BICYCLE ON HILL

REC. BOAT IN WAVES
WAVES "CATCH" FLAT, WIDE BOTTOM

SEA KAYAK IN WAVES
WAVES ROLL UNDER & AROUND

5

Hybrid Recreational Kayaks

Hybrids are combinations of boat designs, such as a rec. boat with a waterproof bulkhead (compartment) similar to a sea kayak. This type of boat can carry some gear, and more importantly, has partial flotation. Keep in mind, though, that the bow (front) of the boat will fill up with water when the boat capsizes, and only the stern (back) will float. Not fun for re-entry! Again, boat design is an issue.

Open cockpit recreational boats and hybrids can be made much safer by the addition of flotation bags so that both the bow (front) and stern (back) will float if the boat capsizes. Inflatable float bags are used by whitewater boaters and can be purchased inexpensively. And, that small cost could save your life!

Most hybrids are fairly inexpensive, although some may have added "bells & whistles". Some specialized hybrids have a paddle wheel for your feet for forward propulsion. Others are designed to attach a sail and/or outrigger.

TIPPING SCENARIOS

Sit-On-Top Recreational Kayaks

These boats are usually plastic, and designed for the paddler to literally sit on top of the boat to paddle. Sit-on-tops are meant to get you out playing on the water, and you can easily climb back on them. They're generally designed for calm water near shore. The kayak itself is totally sealed and water-tight and because there are no openings for water to enter, these boats cannot sink. They can tip over, but righting the boat and re-entry are easy. Many fishing kayaks are sit-on-tops and have a broad, flattened area on the surface of the boat for gear. These boats often do not paddle as easily as other boats however, because wind can easily "push them around".

Note – Whitewater kayaks are not the same as recreational kayaks! They are short, plastic boats, but have a totally different boat design made for rivers. The hull has a lot of "rocker" (front to back, like a rocking chair), and they are almost impossible to paddle straight on non-moving water.

* Remember: All recreational kayaks (rec. boats) are deceptively safe on flat water, but they are the first boats to capsize in larger waves. They can sink or partially sink, making re-entry impossible. Using float bags (inflatable) makes them safer!

Canoes

Canoes are personal watercraft that are entirely or largely open boats with raised seats for the paddlers (although some are designed for a kneeling paddling position). The paddler has a single paddle that is dipped first on one side, then the other for forward propulsion and steering.

Canoes have been popular personal watercraft for ages, but in recent years kayaks appear to have surpassed their popularity. Many canoes are designed to carry the paddler(s) and lots of gear for backcountry camping. Others may be designed for racing or even short outings similar to rec. boats.

Canoes may be made of a variety of materials such as aluminum, wood, fiberglass, and ABS plastic. When capsized, canoes do take on large amounts of water, but most float (at least partially) because of construction. It is possible to re-enter a canoe, but not easily. Again, decide what you want to do with a canoe before purchasing one so you can get the most enjoyment out of it.

SUP'S (Stand-up Paddleboards)

SUP's have exploded in popularity in recent years, and like kayaks, are now available in a variety of shapes and materials, again designed with various purposes in mind. Basically, all of them are boards that you stand on and paddle with a single, bent paddle. Some are designed for flat water, others for waves and surfing. The paddler's weight and skill are determining factors for most SUP's.

One advantage of SUP's is the ability to see more of the horizon because of the standing position. Paddling these boards works the entire body, but especially the core muscles, so often they are used for exercise and cross training. Some folks even do yoga moves on SUP's.

Carrying gear is limited, but some offer the ability to strap gear to the deck. There are even inflatable SUP's, and a new hybrid that allows you to pedal for forward movement. Most have one or more fins (removable or retractable) to help with steering. Cost varies considerably, but most are on the affordable scale, so they're a great way to get out on the water. And, they all float! (Plus, if you fall off, you can easily get back on).

Gear & Clothing

1. Paddles – There's way too much information here for the scope of this book, but a good generality is: Choose your paddle for your boat and paddling style,

and buy the lightest one you can afford! Your arms and shoulders will thank you.

For sea kayaks, a longer, thinner blade is used for low angle paddling, but for the most efficient high angle paddling form, a shorter, wider blade is best. For sea kayaks with a width of less than 24", most people need a 210 cm. paddle for high angle paddling according to the "Werner Paddles" website.

2. <u>PFD</u> – Personal flotation device, or "life jacket" – required by law and previously discussed.

3. <u>Sprayskirt</u> -- For sea kayaks only (and some hybrids), keeps the water out and the paddler in if he/she decides to roll back up after capsizing. Sprayskirts do not "trap you" in a boat as they have a loop at the front that releases them, or they release from the sides.

4. <u>Paddle float & pump</u> – Paddle float acts as an "outrigger" for sea kayaks and hybrids so you can more easily do a solo re-entry. And, of course, the pump gets the water out!

5. <u>Leashes</u> – For a paddle, or a board to keep them with you in case of capsize.

6. <u>Other miscellaneous gear</u> – Includes: sponges, compass, dry bags, map/chart cases, etc.

7. <u>Clothing</u> –
   - Paddle jacket, ideally waterproof or water resistant
   - Paddle pants, "quick dry" pants, or shorts
   - Waterproof or water resistant hat
   - Neoprene booties or sandals (be aware that sandals can catch on kayak pegs)
   - Thermal protective clothing – neoprene "wetsuits" or waterproof dry suits (more expensive).
   - Dry clothing in a dry bag in case of capsize

NORTHWEST MONTANA

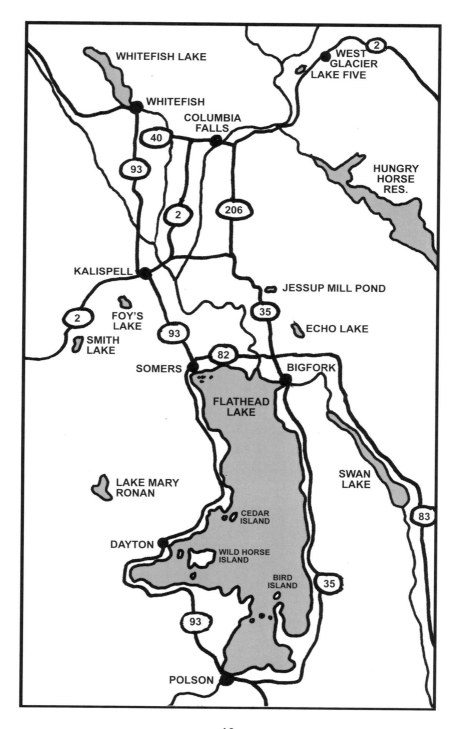

FLATHEAD VALLEY

FOY'S LAKE

Location: 8 min., 3 mi., N. 48.161 – W. 114.351
Paddle Craft: Any
Skill Level: Beginner
Outing: 30 min. – 1.5 hrs.
Launch Facilities: Gravel area adjacent to boat launch, pit toilets, picnic tables
Special Interest: Uninhabited island, swimming area, close to town
Caution: Crowding, wave runners and boat traffic in summer

Directions: Take Hwy. 2 W. of Kalispell and turn left to access the bypass (or turn left earlier onto Meridian Rd.). If you're on the bypass, at the first round-a-bout, take the Foy's Lake Road exit (first one to right). Continue up the hill past the Lone Pine State Park sign and first lake parking area (boat carry is too steep here) to the second, larger parking area that is a Parks and Rec. Lake Access.

FOY'S LAKE

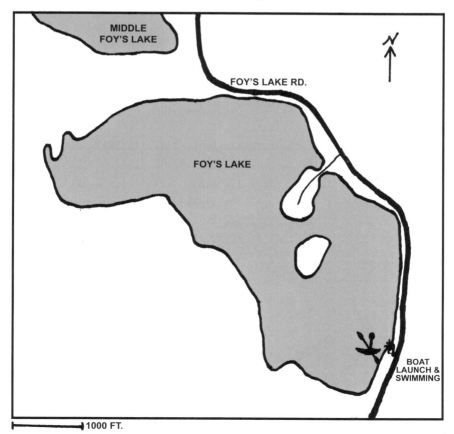

Paddle Notes: Foy's Lake is the closest lake to Kalispell and a great place for beginners. It's not a wild place like many lakes in northwest MT, but the houses and cabins along the lakeshore don't interfere with the lake's charm, especially if you're there early in the morning or in the spring or fall. In mid summer, though, this lake is really crowded and you'll have to compete with boats and wave runners.

A suggested paddle from the launch is counter-clockwise. The island near the middle is a scenic short destination with a clear, shallow bottom on the south end. This is an excellent place to practice boat or board skills, and the water's warmer here. There's a peninsula next to the island, and the area between them, around the west side of the peninsula and the north side of the lake gets less boat traffic. If you paddle on to the northwest end of the lake, there are two shallow bays where birds often hang out, and in the reedy area you might even see turtles and possibly some large goldfish (probably illegally introduced).

From the northwest end, it's a leisurely paddle along the western shoreline where cabins and houses are numerous. If you paddle close to shore, you'll often see kingfishers, mergansers, and other ducks. In early spring and late fall, it's even possible to see loons. The south end of the lake is shallow and has a few reedy areas with more possibility of wildlife. Circumnavigating the lake is about 4 miles, so it's a nice paddling workout if your timing is right.

CHURCH SLOUGH

Location: 20 min., 10 mi., N. 48.149 – W. 114.205
Paddle Craft: Any
Skill Level: Beginners
Outing: 1-1.5 hrs., 2-3 mi. (or, longer time/distance if you choose to access the lower Flathead River)

CHURCH SLOUGH

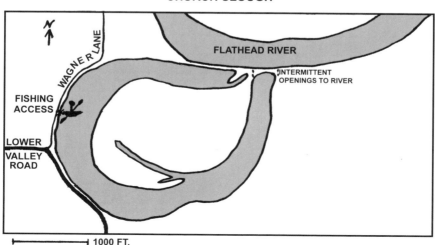

Launch Facilities: Pit toilet, parking area, boat launch
Special Interest: Quiet paddle, lots of birds, great evening/morning paddle
Caution: Wind/waves when storms come up

Directions: Take Hwy. 93 south to the traffic light at a 5-way intersection and take a left on Lower Valley Road. Go about 5 miles to Wagner Lane and turn left. From this turn, it's less than .3 miles to the Church Slough Fishing Access parking area on the right.

Paddle Notes: Church Slough is an old oxbow of the Flathead River. Paddling the slough is much like paddling a lake, but the water does get "renewed" at spring runoff from the narrow river access at the northwest end. It's generally easy to enter the river here, but you will notice a bit of current as you do so. During most of the year (excluding spring) this lower section of the Flathead River has very slow current that's easy to paddle against to return to the slough if you choose to lengthen your outing.

If you paddle to the right (south) from the put-in, you'll find that the slough is relatively wide and has a narrow peninsula in the middle that's fun to paddle behind. It's interesting to explore the shoreline, most of which is uninhabited. There's a few cabins and homes on the slough, but not enough to spoil this peaceful, serene country landscape with awesome views of the Swan range.

There's plenty of wildlife here and you're pretty much guaranteed to see a large variety of both water and shore birds. Eagles and osprey are common, along with a variety of ducks and geese. Fishing is great, and you may also note the occasional river otter, beaver, or mink. This is an ideal early evening paddle with the golden light and alpenglow off the Swan Mountains. And, it's perfect for your first few outings with a new boat/board.

CRESTON JESSUP MILL POND

Location: 25 min., 14mi., N. 48.119 – W. 114.115
Paddle Craft: Any
Skill Level: Beginner
Outing: 30 min. -1.5 hrs.
Launch Facilities: Grassy area on east side of dam, & bridge, restrooms in Hatchery buildings which close at 4pm.
Special Interest: Historical old mill town site, National Fish Hatchery (other side of dam) with crystal clear, cold water. This pond (it's actually larger than a pond) rarely freezes as it's recharged by several large springs, and even on a hot summer's day, the water stays cold!
Caution: Water temperature, even in summer near springs is 40's-50's.

Directions: Head west from Kalispell on Hwy. 2, and at the intersection with Hwy 35, proceed west on Hwy. 35. (Hwy. 2 turns to the left). Continue just past the Hwy. 206 intersection at Woody's store and turn left onto Lake Blaine Rd. Proceed to Creston

Hatchery Rd., turn right and continue south to the Creston Fish Hatchery's small parking lot across the dam. Park and carry boats across the road to the grassy launch area east of the dam and near the picnic table. *Note- not much of the pond is visible from the launch area – it's much bigger than it looks!

JESSUP MILL POND

CRESTON HATCHERY

CRESTON HATCHERY RD.

N

JESSUP MILL POND

PARKING

CRESTON HATCHERY ROAD

DAM

PARKING

KAUFFMAN RD.

1000 FT

Paddle Notes: The Jessup Mill pond name comes from the old Jessup lumber mill, and today, the Creston National Fish Hatchery is located on part of the old mill town and utilizes its exceptional water quality for the hatchery. The area is off the beaten path in the countryside, beautiful and serene. As you paddle east towards the base of the Swan mountains the pond opens up considerably.

The Mill Pond is fed by five large springs and empties into Mill creek at the dam. Because the pond is constantly recharged, the water is unique in that it's always crystal clear, clean, and cold, even midsummer. Often, this is the only open water to be found in early spring or late fall. Glass bottom boat rides come to mind as you enjoy the under water view of huge ancient logs, an old wooden water pipe system, and lacy green plants.

Birds and wildlife are abundant in this serene habitat, and Canada Geese nest here in the spring. Great Blue Herons, eagles, ospreys, and migrating waterfowl are common. Mink can often be seen swimming in the pond.

Close to the end of the pond you'll find a charming tiny island that's only big enough to land one or two boats. If you continue paddling to the end of the pond, there's an old concrete footing and logs that block your passage. If you're quiet, you can usually hear some of the gurgling sounds from the springs.

Before or after your paddle, you might want to tour the Creston Hatchery and read up on the Jessup Mill town history. There's also a short nature trail in the area.

14

ECHO, ABBOTT, & PETERSON LAKES

Location: 30 min., 21 mi. (Hwy. 82) or 22 mi.(Hwy. 35,) N. 48.130 – W. 114.038
Paddle Craft: Any
Skill Level: Beginners
Outing: 2-5 hrs.
Launch Facilities: Gravel beach beside boat launch at fishing area, restrooms
Special Interest: Highly convoluted, interesting shoreline, eagle & osprey nests, 3 lakes with narrow (almost hidden) channel from Echo to Abbott lake, great scenery, and one of the warmest lakes in the valley. This is a great place to practice boat and board skills (rolling, re-entry, etc.). Also eagle & osprey nests
Caution: Boat and wave-runner traffic mid-day and mid-summer

Directions: There are two ways to get to these lakes:

1. Take Hwy. 93 south and turn left at the light and intersection of Hwy. 82. Proceed east to the intersection (light) of Hwy. 35. Take a right, then a quick left at the "Little Brown Church" onto the Swan Hwy. for less than a mile. After the Echo Lake Café, turn left onto Echo Lake Rd. Continue north and stay left at the "Y" with Foothill Rd. You will see the lake and continue over the causeway where the road becomes gravel. Follow the signs for the fishing area and take the left down a hill to the launch.

ECHO LAKE

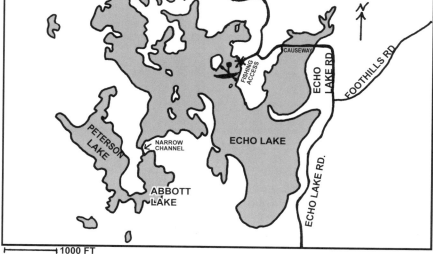

2. Take Hwy. 2 west and then Hwy.35 as it continues west. Continue as the road turns south in Creston after Woody's store (which has great sandwiches and snacks). Turn left on LaBrandt Rd. and continue several miles as it becomes a gravel road at some point. The road really winds a lot as you get closer to the lake. Follow the signs to the fishing access.

Paddle Notes: Echo Lake is spring-fed and relatively shallow, so it's often one of the first lakes you can paddle in the spring. And, when the Swan mountains are still snow-covered, the scenery is breathtaking! Fall is amazing as well with some snow on the peaks and full color on the shoreline. A complete circumnavigation of all three lakes could take most of a day (about 15 miles for all 3), and just Echo lake with all its' nooks & crannies could take several hours. There are several islands and numerous peninsulas and bays.

The two most interesting paddles involve exploring the Echo Lake bays to the northwest, and paddling to Abbott and Peterson Lakes. The route to these other two lakes is the route described.

ECHO LAKE

The bay and island immediately to the right of the launch is worth exploring as it's particularly serene, close, and a great place to practice paddling skills. From the south end of the island near this bay (and the launch), proceed directly across the lake. Paddle west towards the islands you see in the distance, and as you get closer, you'll notice a large eagle's nest to the right. Continue paddling towards the end of the bay. To the right of a large home near the end of the bay you'll see the narrow channel that connects the lakes. It's hard to see until you're right on it! In the spring and during most of the summer, this channel will accommodate small to medium-sized motorized boats. But, towards late summer and fall, the channel is not as deep, and by early fall only kayaks, canoes, and SUP's have access. Wahoo!

The channel is a few hundred feet long and winds to the right. It opens into Abbott lake, a small lake with fewer houses. Continue paddling past a picnic table and small pavilion on the left (private property) and just past the peninsula and "pinch point" you'll enter Peterson Lake. This lake also has fewer houses, and there's a private camp at the north end. Sometimes there's a water skiing slalom course set north to south in this lake, and if there's no boat traffic, you can practice your turns.

On the way back, notice the large osprey nest on the point of the last peninsula prior to crossing to the launch. Because it's relatively shallow, this lake is a great fishing hole for eagles and ospreys. Kingfishers are also common and you can often see loons in the spring and fall (when there's less boat traffic.) The birds and scenery certainly won't disappoint you on Echo lake!

SMITH LAKE

Location: 20 min., 12 mi., N. 48.108 – W. 114.441
Paddle Craft: Any
Skill Level: Beginner
Outing: 1-2 hrs.
Launch Facilities: Gravel parking area, pit toilet
Special Interest: Outstanding bird watching area! Sandhill cranes in spring

SMITH LAKE

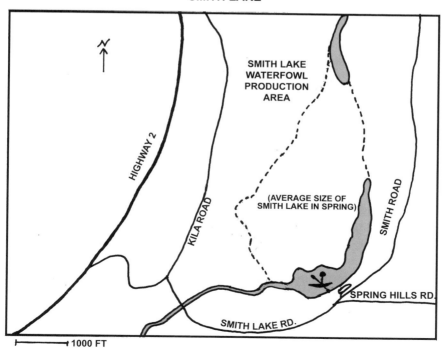

Caution: Lake is much smaller as summer progresses, best time to paddle is spring, and that's when there are more birds and wildlife

Directions: Take Hwy. 2 West about 8 miles and turn left onto Kila Rd. at an intersection with a bar/restaurant with a large mural on the side. Continue on Kila Rd. past the town of Kila to the intersection of Smith Lake Rd. Take a left onto Smith Lake road, go over Ashley Creek and continue left past Browns Meadow Rd. to the gravel parking area at the south end of the lake (just past Spring Hill Rd. Intersection).

Paddle Notes: This little lake gets much larger with spring runoff, so it's recommended primarily for spring and early summer paddling. Hundreds of species of migrating birds pass through this valley, and Smith Lake is a waterfowl production area. So, bring your binoculars!

In the spring, Smith Lake is a bird lovers' paradise, especially when the Sandhill cranes are migrating. These birds are huge – over three feet tall with wide wingspans and blue-grayish coloring with white and red (males) on top of their heads. Seeing one is a real treat, and an experience you likely won't forget!

From the parking area, you can easily circumnavigate the lake, which is only a mile or two and is a popular fishing spot for perch and pike. In the spring, there's usually plenty of water to paddle up Ashley creek and under the bridge, and this makes the paddle longer and more fun. There's not much current to paddle against, and you can often paddle for a mile with great scenery and plenty of wildlife. There's an abundant diversity of shorebirds and nesting waterfowl, including: wood ducks, bitterns, grebes, flycatchers, swans, and great blue herons. The predatory birds are present as well, so look for ospreys, hawks, and eagles.

WHITEFISH LAKE

Location: 35 min., 18 mi., City Beach: N. 48.417 – W. 114.352
Paddle Craft: Any for river; sea kayaks, canoes or SUP's (advanced) for crossing
Skill Level: Beginner for river paddle, advanced beginner for lake crossing
Outing: 1-3 hrs., 2-5 miles depending on paddle choice
Launch Facilities: City Beach, Les Mason Park, and River Trail Park - gravel or grassy launch areas, pit toilets, parking facilities
Special Interest: lazy river or scenic lake paddling with Big Mountain backdrop
Caution: River current in spring, wind/waves on lake

Directions: (City Beach) Take Hwy. 93 N. to Whitefish and turn left onto W. 2nd St. Go two blocks and turn right on Wisconsin Ave. over the viaduct. Take the first left on E. Edgewood Dr. and follow this road to the end as it curves around to Lakeside Blvd. and takes you to Whitefish City Beach, a city park and the launch area.

Paddle Notes: From City Beach, there are several destinations to paddle, and all can be done one way with a shuttle if you choose:

- Whitefish River Paddle: (N. 48.407 – W. 114.339) Paddle from City Beach to River Trail Park off Baker Ave. (about 1.5 mi.). From the sandy launch at the park, paddle to the left (southeast) and around a point to the lake outflow which is the beginning of the Whitefish River. Generally, the current is slow, but it can be a quick, fun ride at the beginning. Then the current slows to the point where it

WHITEFISH LAKE

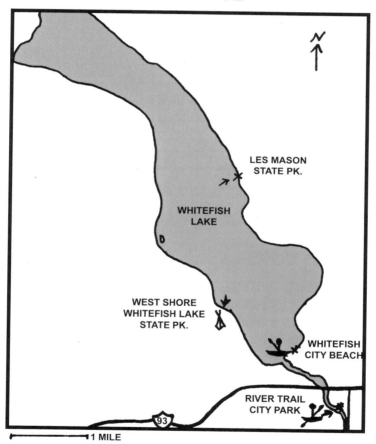

seems like a long narrow lake. In the next 1.5 miles you'll travel a very peaceful, lazy river with lots of shady tree cover. Ducks and geese are plentiful and there's a section about 2/3 of the way down that opens up into a marshy area with cattails and red-winged blackbirds. The take-out at the park (co-ordinates above) is an easily visible grassy area, and it's only a short carry to the parking lot if you've shuttled. Or you can paddle back to City Beach. It's easy to portage at the lake opening where there's more current.

- West Shore Whitefish Lake St. Campground:
(N. 48.426 – W. 114.372) Paddle to the left of the launch and past the Whitefish River outflow, following the shoreline up the west side of the lake to West Shore Park and campground. There's a small shallow bay at the park, and the take-out is easy, but can be muddy. Both picnic tables and restrooms are available. If you choose to continue up the west side, in less than a mile you'll come to another small bay with a quaint little island. Round trip is only 3-4 mi.

- Les Mason Park: (N. 48.458 – W. 114.373) Although it's possible to paddle the shoreline to the right of the launch, most folks choose to do an open water crossing to the park. As an open crossing, it's a two mile paddle to the north. Les Mason is a small park located off Lakeshore Drive and has a nice grassy picnic area with a few tables and a restroom. This state park doesn't get a lot of use except during mid-summer, so it's generally quiet and a good picnic destination.

TALLY LAKE

Location: 50 min., 26 mi., N. 48.412 – W. 114.582
Paddle Craft: Any
Skill Level: Advanced beginner
Outing: 2-4 hrs.
Launch Facilities: Boat launch at a small bay with a good gravel beach, good parking and restrooms – fee area for parking and launch
Special Interest: This is the deepest natural lake in MT- 492 ft. with interesting rocks and cliffy areas. Also, possible backcountry kayak/canoe camping as well as the main Forest Service campground
Caution: Cold water, even mid-summer, wind in afternoons, $4.00 parking fee

Directions: Take Hwy. 2 west to the first traffic light after the bypass. This is W. Springcreek Rd., and you'll take a right and continue until the intersection of Farm to Market Rd. (424). Turn right on Farm to Market and proceed for at least 10 miles until the road does a quick jog to the left, then back right and you see the Tally Lake sign. Turn left and follow the Tally Lake gravel road. You will see rock formations and glimpses of the lake on the right side of the road before you come to the campground area. Turn right into the campground where there is a gate and a $4.00 fee/vehicle. Follow the signs to the boat launch.

Paddle Notes:

Circumnavigating is a great way to experience this gem of a lake. Going clockwise, you'll start off near the stream inflow for the lake, and you might notice that the already cold water gets much colder after the stream enters with its mountain runoff.

TALLY LAKE

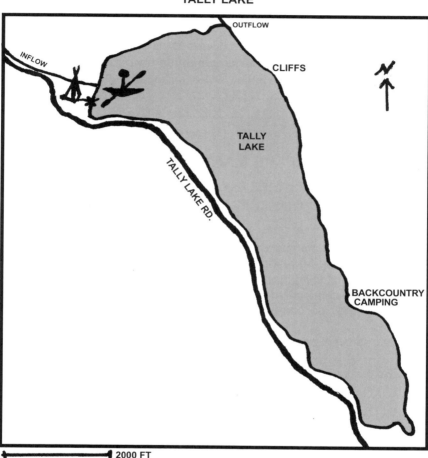

Continue paddling to the north side of the lake where the lake outflows and you'll find a bit of current. It's fun to paddle down a ways, but you can't go far because of the rocky, shallow bottom. Paddling onward, you'll come to some picturesque and colorful cliffs on the northeast side of the lake. With the cliffs and the deep sapphire blue of the lake, you'll want to grab the camera.

As you continue south towards the end of the lake, you'll encounter a small bay where you can take out on the side of a short peninsula. There are several backcountry campsites in this area, and it's a great place to walk around and stretch your legs or have lunch. Backcountry camping is permitted here as it's Forest Service land, so Forest Service regulations apply, but there's no fee.

At the end of the lake there's a small bay and another take out area for lunch, fishing, etc. It's approximately 3 miles to the end of the lake. On the way back, there's more rock walls and forested shores before you get back to the launch.

Tally Lake and the campground can get crowded in the summer, but if you paddle early in the morning, or in the spring or fall you can often have the lake to yourself. Aside from being the deepest lake in Montana, it's definitely one of the prettiest outside of Glacier National Park.

LAKE MARY RONAN

Location: 45 min., 37 mi., N. 47.925 – W. 114.386 (This lake is not technically in the Flathead Valley, but is close.)
Paddle Craft: Any
Skill Level: Beginner
Outing: 1-3 hrs. (2-3 hrs. for circumnavigation)
Launch Facilities: Lake Mary Ronan State Park and campground fishing access-parking, boat launch, pit toilet, grassy/gravel area for launch
Special Interest: Exceptional area for fishing and birds. Great blue herons and cormorants! (Yes, they do come inland!) Moose often frequent the area and swim across the lake.
Caution: Boat traffic mid-day, mid-summer

Directions: Take Hwy. 93 south from Kalispell to Dayton and turn right at the sign for Lake Mary Ronan. It's about 7 miles to the lake. Follow the signs to Lake Mary Ronan State Park where there's parking at the fishing launch.

Paddle Notes: Circumnavigating the lake is about 6-8 mi., and the paddle described goes clockwise from the launch. To the south (left) of the launch is a long, reedy shoreline where there's plenty of aquatic bird activity. About half way to the south end of the lake is Camp Tuffit where you may want to stop after the paddle to get ice cream, pie, etc. at the "Crawdad Shack." This is a private, small and rustic resort, but the food area is open to the public. It's barely noticeable as you paddle by because it's quaint and blends in well with the forested and reedy shoreline.

The south end of the lake is a marsh with reeds and cattails that are repeated at the west and north sides where there is inflow. These marshes make the area an outstanding habitat for aquatic birds, and it's not uncommon to see as many as a dozen Great Blue Herons on an outing. Additionally, moose are often spotted on the lake feeding on aquatic plants or swimming across the lake.

As you continue along the northwest shoreline of the lake (about ¾ of the way around the lake if you're circumnavigating), watch for two tall, dead trees where cormorants hang out. At least a dozen of these normally oceanic birds were observed on the spring day the paddle occurred. What a treat!

LAKE MARY RONAN

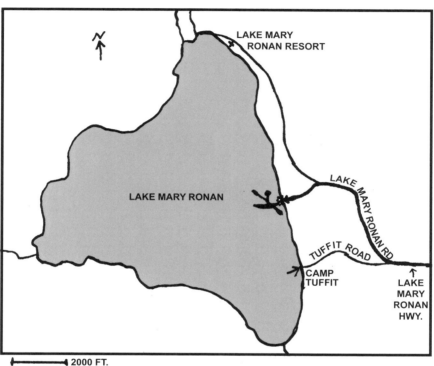

And, speaking of treats, The Lake Mary Ronan Resort at the north/northeast end of the lake is a great place for a meal or drinks, although it was closed for remodeling at the time of the paddle. At least Camp Tuffit was open, though, and the cherry pie was a great reward at the Crawdad Shack! The camp is accessible both by boat and as a short drive by taking a right as you start to leave on the Lake Mary Ronan Highway. And, for the perfect ending to your day, there's a lakeside pavilion and picnic tables where you can enjoy your goodies.

FLATHEAD LAKE MARINE TRAIL

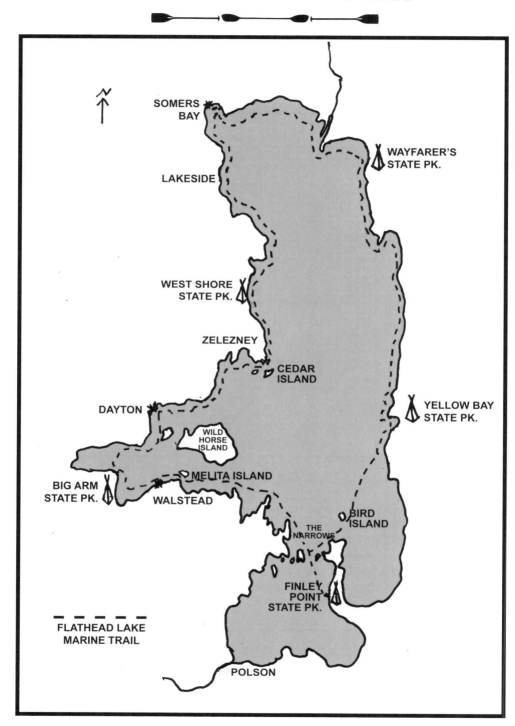

FLATHEAD LAKE

Flathead Lake is the largest fresh water lake west of the Mississippi R. (by surface area), and one of the cleanest, most beautiful and pristine lakes in the country. The water is crystal clear and has an amazing range of colors from royal blue to aquas and emerald greens depending on the location and depth. This lake was glacier carved thousands of years ago and is 27miles long and up to 15.5 miles wide. It averages 165 ft. deep with a maximum depth of 370 ft. On the east side, the Swan mountains form a perfect backdrop for this majestic lake. And, even on a midsummer's day, this lake is far less crowded than most lakes in the country because of the low population density in northwest Montana.

There is an established Flathead Lake Marine trail where paddlers can paddle the entire lake or sections of the lake between state parks. A few tent campsites are reserved for marine trail paddlers and are filled on a first come, first serve basis. The campsites are at the following state parks going counter-clockwise from Somers Bay at the northwest part of the lake: West Shore, Big Arm, Finley Point, Yellow Bay, and Wayfarer's.

Additional public launching sites for the lake are at: Somers Bay, Lakeside City Park, Zelezney (state access), Dayton, Walstead (fishing access), Riverside Park in Polson, and Flathead River (fishing access) in Bigfork. There is more public access on the west side of the lake than the east where there are an abundance of cherry orchards. The famous Flathead cherries are generally harvested in July.

Please use caution when paddling Flathead Lake as winds generally come up in the afternoon (prevailing southwesterlies). They can come up quickly and with the long fetch of such a huge lake, waves can get dangerously high. These waves can capsize medium to large powerboats, let alone personal watercraft. Remember also that Flathead Lake is cold all summer except in a few shallow bays next to shore, so always wear your PFD zipped and snugged.

FLATHEAD LAKE, PAINTED ROCKS AREA

SOMERS BAY

Location: 15 min., 7 mi., Somers beach (swim area): N 48.078 – W. 114.234
Paddle Craft: Any
Skill Level: Beginners, ideal practice area for skills, any level
Outing: 1-2 hrs., 2-3 mi.
Launch Facilities: Pit toilets, gravel beach, good parking (except mid-summer weekends because of overflow parking by power boaters)
Special Interest: Utterly charming, picturesque bay at the north end of Flathead Lake with: several islands, a dilapidated wooden building, sailboats, historic dock posts, ospreys and eagles, and less boat traffic because of shallow water (which makes the water warmer in summer) Terrific place for beginners, skills practice
Caution: Wind/waves past islands in bay

SOMER'S BAY

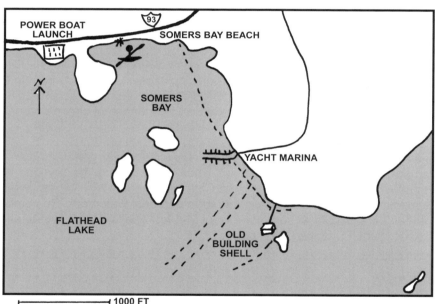

Directions: Take Hwy. 93 south for 7 miles to the Northwest end of Flathead Lake in Somers, past mm. 103. Turn left to the launch at the first turn, before you get to the power boat launch and parking area. There is a swimming beach here with a roped off area in the summer, but you can launch on either side.

Paddle Notes: Somers Bay is a little gem of a paddling area with a backdrop of the rugged Swan Mountains, the sapphire blue lake, and a foreground of several small rocky islands with ospreys soaring overhead. Sailboats docked at the marina on the far left add extra ambiance to the scene. With easy access and a gentle gravel beach to launch, Somers Bay is an ideal spot for your first time in a kayak, canoe, or SUP, or just a leisurely outing with plenty of great scenery. And, there's few problems with boat traffic or wave runners as the bay is relatively shallow.

As you launch outside the swimming area, there are four islands you can easily circumnavigate (all are private). Watch for the osprey nest on the first one to the left and a Lilliputian cabin on the smallest island. Old wooden dock posts are a reminder of days gone by when Somers was busy with logging operations. A ferry transported passengers and goods from Polson when roads around the lake were primitive. You can thread your way through the ragged wooden relics of the old ferry dock as you paddle. Today, they serve as territorial perches for the seagulls. Once past the old dock remains, there's a wooden shell of a building with broken windows that's been stabilized on steel girders and currently is home to swallows in the summer. Evidently, at one time it was slated to be a restaurant.

Photo Courtesy of Jim Pederson

SOMERS BAY

Adjacent to the wooden structure, there's another small island (also privately owned). Once past this island, you'll see a small crossing to the last island that's out of the bay area and sits in the main body of Flathead Lake. The crossing to this island is less than .5 mile, but can be treacherous in high winds. If the weather's good, though, it's worth the paddle. There's a shallow, flat rocky shelf on the left side of this state-owned island where you can land if you wish to explore. Most of the island is open rock with some vegetation, and geese use the island as a nesting spot. (Watch out for the goose poop)! At the south end, there's a nice cliff face and elevated lake view that makes a great picnic spot. And, the crystal clear deep blue water below makes for fine swimming on a hot sunny day. Somers Bay is also an exceptional evening paddle with golden lighting on the sailboats, islands, and old wooden posts from the former docks.

WAYFARER'S PARK

Location: 40 min., 22 mi., N. 48.054 – W 114.081
Paddle Craft: Any
Skill Level: Beginner
Outing: 30 min.-2 hrs.
Launch Facilities: Parking, boat launch, pit toilets
Special Interest: Bigfork Bay, Flathead river delta area
Caution: Potential high current in Bigfork Bay, shallow areas around river mouth

WAFARER'S PARK

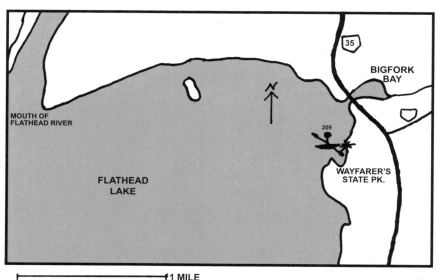

Directions: Go south on Hwy. 93 to the traffic light intersection and turn left onto Hwy. 82 near Somers. Continue on Hwy. 82 to the Hwy. 35 intersection and turn right. Proceed past the Swan River bridge crossing in Bigfork and turn right into Wayfarer's Park at the sign less than a half mile after the bridge.

Paddle Notes: Wayfarer's park will delight you with it's huge rocks adjacent to the lake, wildflowers, and hiking trails to the left of the boat launch. There's also a shaded large picnic area to the right. The views of the Swan Mountains are spectacular here, and the short bay in front of the picnic tables is protected from winds and a great place for novice paddlers. Paddlefest, an annual paddling event is held here each year on the third weekend of May.

From the launch area, there are three main venues for paddling:

- Bigfork Bay: Paddle northeast less than a quarter mile to the Hwy. 35 bridge which opens into the small bay adjacent to the village of Bigfork. Accessibility is determined by water flow from the Swan River, and the current is literally the gate-keeper. Best access is from mid-summer to fall. (During spring run-off, it can be almost impossible and dangerous to paddle into the bay with the swift currents and eddies around the concrete bridge supports). This bay's not very large, but it's an easy scenic paddle. At any time of year there's a bit of current at the east end because the Swan River enters under the one lane bridge at the village.

WAYFARER'S PARK – PADDLEFEST

- <u>Flathead River mouth and delta</u>: To access this area, paddle north from the launch site and follow the shoreline for approximately three miles. The delta peninsula extends into Flathead Lake almost a mile, and is quite scenic with a few small islands scattered near the tip. This area is shallow in places because of the sediment carried by the river, and will be muddy at spring run-off. Current is minimal most of the time, but can be an issue in the spring. Bald eagles are common and nest in this region along with abundant waterfowl, so consider binoculars and cameras.

- <u>South towards boat launch:</u> As you paddle to the left of the launch site, you'll enter the open water of Flathead lake and pass the huge rocks that are such a scenic part of Wayfarer's Park. This rocky hillside extends approximately .5 mile as you paddle south until you reach the park boundary. Flathead Lake Lodge (private) is directly south of the park, and then there's a number of lake homes and private property until you reach a boat launch/fishing area off West View Drive. This area is approximately 4 miles south of the park and provides a take-out area and public restrooms.

CEDAR ISLAND & PAINTED ROCKS

Location: 30 min., 23 mi., Zelezney launch: N 47.90 1– W 114.171, Cedar Island landing: N. 47.897 – W. 114.167
Paddle Craft: All except rec. boats, longer craft for windy conditions
Skill Level: Intermediate
Outing: 2 -4 hrs. (for both areas, hiking possible), 2 hrs. (Cedar Island only), Round trip to both is approximately 5 miles.
Launch Facilities: Gravel beach, very limited parking, (4 spaces) with private property both sides, no pit toilet or power boat launch
Special Interest: Old homestead on Cedar Is., petroglyphs, soaring cliffs
Caution: Painted Rocks area & East side Cedar Island – wind/waves. Also, old homestead is in danger of collapse.

CEDAR ISLAND & PAINTED ROCKS

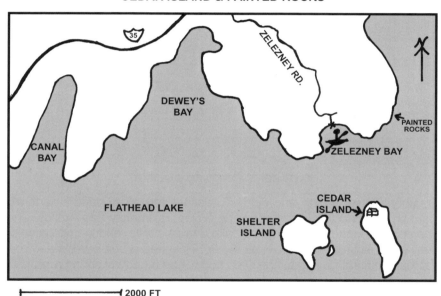

Directions: Take Hwy. 93 S. to mm. 90 and turn left on Zelezney Rd. (look for left turn lane on 93). Continue on dirt road and watch for Zelezney signs on trees at next two intersections. Keep left at Osprey Loop intersection, and turn right at the next "Y". Look for rail fence and tennis court to the left of the road, and keep proceeding along blacktop ass it curves left. Then (quickly), turn right down towards the lake on steep gravel. Parking area only holds 4 vehicles, but some are long spots, so you could park behind friends.

Paddle Notes:
- Cedar, Shelter Islands: Cedar Island is public land and is a half-mile paddle from Zelezney. There's a small, sheltered boat landing/gravel beach below the old homestead and on the left side of the island. A trail to the left takes you to

the dilapidated old house and moss covered outbuildings. Caution is advised on entering this unstable structure with so many rotten boards.

From the homestead, there's a trail to an old orchard and the other end of the island. There are no restroom facilities on the island. It's a little over a mile to circumnavigate the island if you choose. On the east side behind the old homestead you'll find a short gravel beach that's partially protected by rocks.

CEDAR ISLAND HOMESTEAD LANDING

As you paddle towards the south end of the island, it's a short jaunt to a tiny, rocky middle island, and then a short distance to Shelter Island. Shelter is privately owned as you'll note from the "no trespassing" signs; massive, castle like home; and elaborate boat house. The three islands together make for a short, picturesque, and interesting paddle.

• Painted Rocks- The painted rocks are petroglyphs on a cliff face drawn in a reddish pigment and depicting various animals. There's also a series of hash marks that likely mark animals taken by early native tribes.

To access the painted rocks from Zelezney, simply paddle left along the shore to the north point of Zelezney bay. Once you round this tip, it's more exposed and usually rougher water, and it's another half mile north to the pictographs. This is the only high cliffy area on the lake and it's spectacular with colorful rock faces interspersed with bonsai-like trees. Access from Cedar Island involves a half-mile crossing to the point.

There's not a place to land, but you can paddle fairly close to the cliff face if the water's calm and enjoy the petroglyphs. They're located above a shelf that's 4-6 ft. above the water line. The entire petroglyph area is only about 20-30 ft. wide, so watch carefully for it as you paddle.

WILD HORSE ISLAND

Location: 45 min., 38 mi. to Dayton: N. 47.865 – W. 114.272, landing site Skeeko Bay: N. 47.847 – W. 114.234
Paddle Craft: Longer (15' or more) sea kayak with spray skirt. No rec. boats, and crossing is not recommended for open cockpit, shorter kayaks or canoes because of high wind & waves that come up quickly on crossings.
Skill Level: High intermediate only!
Outing: 3-6 hrs., depending on hiking time & trip. Round trip to Skeeko Bay is 4-5 mi., circumnavigation is 12 mi.
Launch Facilities: Grassy & gravel launch area at end of "B" St.. * Make sure to park vehicles up the street by field. There's a pit toilet at the far end of the field, and also a solar composting toilet on Wild Horse ¼ mi. from Skeeko Bay.

WILD HORSE ISLAND

![Map of Wild Horse Island showing Dayton, "B" Street, Highway 93, Cromwell Island, Skeeko Bay, Wild Horse Island, Flathead Lake, and Melita Island. Scale: 2000 FT.]

Special Interest: Hiking, incredible views, 5 wild horses, large herd of bighorn sheep & spectacular rams, deer, wildflowers
Caution: High wind and waves often develop in afternoon, especially on the east side of the island and the crossing back to Dayton. This crossing on return is often very

challenging/grueling, and drownings have occurred here. It's best to wait until winds die down in early evening if you're caught on the island when the wind picks up.

Directions: Take Hwy. 93 south on the west shore of Flathead Lake to the small sailing community of Dayton. Turn left off of Hwy 93 at the Lake Mary Ronan exit past mm. 83. Proceed to the first intersection and turn right. Go one block to B street and turn left. You'll drive past a field on the right and then several dry dock sailboats. The launch is at the end of B St.

WILD HORSE ISLAND SPRING SHORELINE

Paddle Notes: Wild Horse is the largest island in Flathead Lake, and has the highest elevation. The state of Montana purchased Wild Horse Island and put the majority of the land back in the public domain several years ago, although a few cottages were "grandfathered" in and remain private on the south and east sides. The island gets its name from stories of early Indian tribes stashing their horses on the island as a way of safekeeping them from marauding bands.

Today, only 5 horses remain on the island. In contrast, there's a large herd of bighorn sheep and a number of deer. There are no predators or hunting on the island, so some of the bucks and rams have huge racks. Late fall is a great time to visit as the bighorn sheep enter the "rut" and head-butting clashes can be heard for long distances.

It's advisable to check wind forecasts before paddling to Wild Horse, and start out early. To access the island in the most protected manner, start paddling towards Cromwell Island and "skirt the shore" northward to the tip and the channel between the islands. Cromwell is a privately owned island, so note the "no trespassing" signs. From the northwest tip of Cromwell, it's about a half-mile crossing to the southwest tip of Wild Horse, and then about the same distance as you continue paddling north around the tip and into Skeeko Bay. The bay is somewhat protected from wind and is a popular overnight mooring for sailboats. This is a great landing/picnic spot with gravel and logs on the beach, and the island trail system starts here. There's a modern compost toilet a quarter mile up the trail, and if you continue hiking, there's the remains of an old homestead and orchard. In late spring and early summer, the Bitterroot (state flower) provide pink carpets for the hillsides, and it's worth the steep hike to the top of the trail for a spectacular view of the entire lake.

If you choose to circumnavigate the island, check the wind direction and paddle accordingly so that you'll have the wind to your back on the last leg of the journey when you're tired. It's typical to encounter whitecaps on the more exposed east side of the island. There are several more beach landings, and one particularly nice one at the northwest tip of the island with plenty of driftwood logs. On the east side of the island, watch out for a rocky section slightly to the northeast that's often a hangout for the big rams. You'll gradually see some signs of civilization with the few cabins left on the island, but most of the paddle will reward you with a feeling of wildness and some spectacular lake scenery.

WALSTEAD & SOUTH SHORE

Location: 45 min., 47 mi. N. 47.812 – W. 114.266
Paddle Craft: Sea kayak, canoe, SUP, rec. boats not recommended
Skill Level: Advanced beginner
Outing: 1-3 hrs.
Launch Facilities: Pit toilets, gravel beach, boat launch, good parking
Special Interest: Interesting shoreline, small, hidden cove in Cat Bay, Melita Island and Wild Horse Island if paddling north.
Caution: Wind/waves, especially in afternoon

Directions: Take Hwy. 93 South past Elmo and Big Arm for 47 mi. There's a sign on the Hwy. before the Walstead fishing area, and one at the left turn towards the lake.

Paddle Notes: There's plenty of room to launch on gravel or grass near the parking area and slightly away from the boat ramp. Melita Island could be a short destination paddle and circumnavigation if you don't choose to paddle the entire south shore. Melita is only a half-mile or so off shore and is owned by the Boy Scouts of America, so there are no public landing sites. It's also possible to paddle to Wild Horse Island if you continue past Melita Island.

The main route entails paddling east (right) from the launch point at Walstead. There are some homes along the south shore, but there are fewer as you paddle further. Once you pass the first point that dips sharply south, there are a few short gravel beaches and flat rocky areas that make nice landing spots. If you continue on to the second large point that dips south, you'll enter Cat Bay towards the south end.

There's a delightful, narrow (and almost hidden) cove that was created by drainage from a small interior lake. The cove is shown at the arrow on the map and these coordinates: N. 47.788 – W. 114.246. Once you find the cove, pull in a bit past the rocky bottom (great for swimming in the summer) and there's a small grassy landing

WALSTEAD & SOUTH SHORE

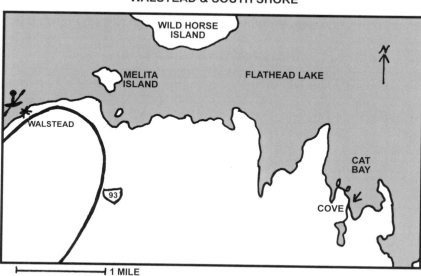

area that will hold several kayaks. One side of the cove is a really narrow peninsula that's fun to hike around and is the beginning of a short hiking trail that may lead to the inner lake. If you choose to paddle on to the Narrows, it's just past the third point.

THE NARROWS & BIRD ISLAND

Location: 1 hr., Finley Point Park: 47 mi., N. 47.756 – W. 114.085
Paddle Craft: Sea kayaks, canoes, SUP's -- rec. boats not recommended
Skill Level: Advanced beginner
Outing: 2-4 hrs.
Launch Facilities: Campground, good parking, launch near or on boat ramp, restroom facilities
Special Interest: Numerous rocky, forested islands, (some with quaint cabins), interesting shoreline, Bird Island
Caution: Wind/waves, especially in afternoon

Directions: Take Hwy. 93 south towards Somers, then turn left on Hwy. 82 at the intersection and head towards Bigfork. At the intersection of Hwy. 35, turn right (south) and proceed around 20 miles to Finley Point. Turn right at the sign onto Finley Point Road. This road veers to the right after a half mile, and then you turn left onto S. Finley Point Rd. Continue to Finley Point State Park.

Paddle Notes: There are two paddles from Finley Point - "The Narrows" which is a series of islands at the narrow entrance to Polson Bay, and Bird Island to the north.

"The Narrows": It's always more fun to paddle amongst islands and convoluted shorelines because you never know what you might see around the point or at the other side of an island. And, that's exactly what you get in this paddle of "the Narrows," the area north of Polson where Flathead Lake pinches in to form Polson Bay.

THE NARROWS & BIRD ISLAND

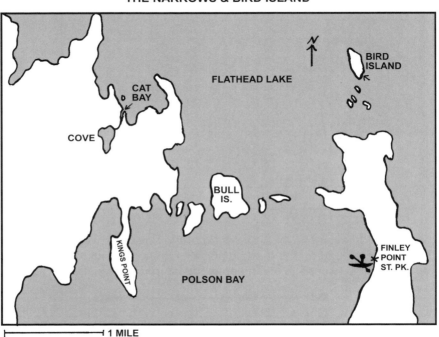

This area can also be accessed from Polson, but the closest, easiest access is Finley Point as described. From Finley Point campground, paddle to the right and the first point you see. Then you can head west about a quarter mile to the first of several islands. The first two are small, and one of them is supposedly a research station, so please adhere to the "no trespassing signs."

There are several cabins and houses, mostly on Bull Island and Little Bull Island, but not enough to distract from the picturesque trees, rocks, and cliffs. As you head further west to the "mainland," you can go south to Kings Point or north to Cat Bay and a small, secluded cove also described in the Walstead, S. Shore paddle. It's easy to miss, so check your GPS for N. 47.788 – W. 114.146. It's a great place for a stretch break or picnic, and makes a good swimming hole in the summer. The lake needs to be full, however, as it's dry when the lake is low.

Bird island: To access this Island, paddle right after launching and continue north past the first point until you get to the northern end of Finley Point. There are homes along the shore, but it's still a pleasant paddle. From the tip of Finley Point, head north to the small islets and islands you see which are directly south of Bird Island. They're fun to paddle around, and eventually you'll reach your destination. There's a small landing on the south side of Bird Island, and a few trails if you're interested in exploring. There are no restroom facilities on the island, so be prepared to "dig a hole". The small beach is a welcome lunch spot looking out at the islands and the Swan Mountains.

FLATHEAD RIVER TO KERR DAM

Location: 55 min., 52 mi., N. 47.694 – W. 114.166
Paddle Craft: Any
Skill Level: Beginner
Outing: 2 hrs.
Launch Facilities: City park with boat and grassy launch site, restrooms
Special Interest: Varied shoreline, Kerr Dam
Caution: Boat traffic in narrow channel, wind (Paddling over the dam is not an issue as It's cabled off a few hundred yards before the end for safety reasons).
*This area is very busy during the summer, and weekends and mid-day are not recommended.

FLATHEAD RIVER TO KERR DAM

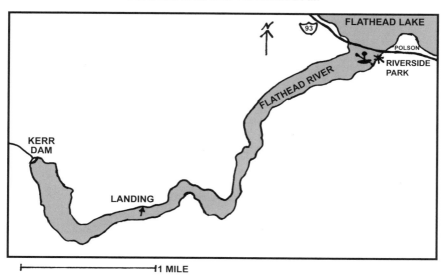

Directions: Take Hwy. 93 south to Polson from Kalispell (fastest, most direct route), or Hwy. 35 south. From Hwy. 93, Riverside Park is across the bridge over the Flathead River (where the lake empties into the river) and is visible to the right. Turn right on the first street after the bridge to access the park.

Paddle Notes: From the launch, paddle to the left and down river towards the dam (about 3-4 mi.) There is very little current in this section of the river and it will feel more like a lake. There are some homes close to Polson, but most of the paddle is scenic with a combination of trees and open land. Fishermen like this area as do water skiers, so watch for boat traffic. Spring and fall are good times to do this paddle, as summer is really busy.

Before the last bend in the river, there's a good landing spot for a picnic on the right that's a bit flat and sandy with a few bushes and trees around. There are some other areas to land, but they're relatively small and not as interesting.

If you paddle as far as you can, there's a cable across the river a few hundred yards from the dam where you'll need to turn around. There's no shuttling involved on this paddle as you return to the launch at the park.

GLACIER NATIONAL PARK

Glacier National Park has it all – spectacular snow-covered jagged peaks, glacier-carved U shaped valleys, the full complement of wildlife including wolves and grizzly bears, and some of the prettiest lakes on the planet. The 7 lakes profiled here (two are considered as Many Glacier Lakes) are the most accessible by vehicle or by hiking trails. (Although Kintla and Bowman Lakes can't be called easily accessible with winding, washboard, and dirt roads). Hiking trails are shown on the maps as they are on one or both sides of the lakes and offer extra recreation possibilities.

The easiest lake to access in the park is Lake McDonald at Apgar, but that also makes it the most crowded. With that said, however, probably less than 1% of tourists in the park actually paddle the lakes, so it's likely that there will be less than 30-50 people on the lake at any given time (paddling). And, it's a large lake, so it won't seem crowded. The Many Glacier Lakes and Two Medicine Lake are next on the list in terms of accessibility and paddling opportunity (read – the wind)! St. Mary's Lake is crown jewel of the park for paddling, but opportunities for a calm day are few, and only skirted sea kayaks with intermediate paddlers should attempt this lake because of potentially dangerous wind and waves.

If you visit Glacier Park, make some special memories through paddling. You'll get away from the crowds and experience the full majesty of this special place. Enjoy!

LAKE McDONALD

GLACIER NATIONAL PARK

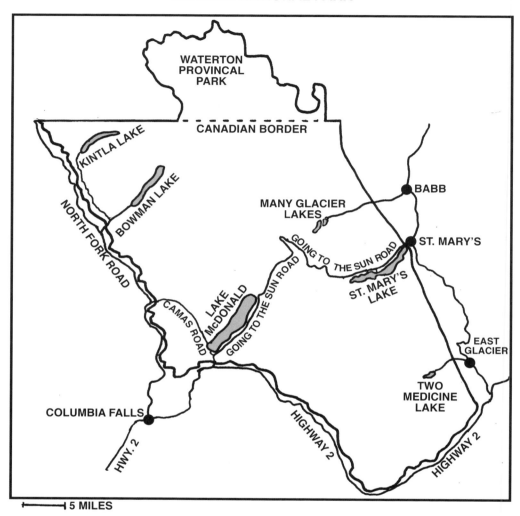

Note: Only lakes listed in this book are shown on this map.

LAKE McDONALD

Locations: 1. Apgar: 1 hr., 50 mi., N. 48.529 – W. 113.992.
2. Fish Creek: 1 hr. 10 min., 52 mi., N. 48.5546 – W. 113.983
3. Back Country campground: N. 48.594 – W. 113.925
Paddle Craft: Any with exception of recreational kayaks- not recommended
Skill Level: Advanced beginner-intermediate
Outing: 1. Apgar to Rocky Point: 2-3 hrs.,
2. Fish Creek to backcountry campground: 2 -3 hrs. (one way)
Launch Facilities: Apgar & Fish Creek- restrooms, parking, boat dock at Apgar
Special Interest: Old wooden tour boat "skeleton" in bay near Rocky Point, Backcountry campground in burned area, gorgeous mountain backdrop, old cabins and homesteads
Caution: Wind/waves can come up in 3-5 minutes, especially in the afternoon and can quickly swamp recreational boats, SUP's, and canoes. Because this lake is the one most often paddled in the park, it bears repeating: ALWAYS WEAR YOUR PFD zipped and snugged! Water is also very cold, so consider thermal protection. And, remember,

LAKE McDONALD

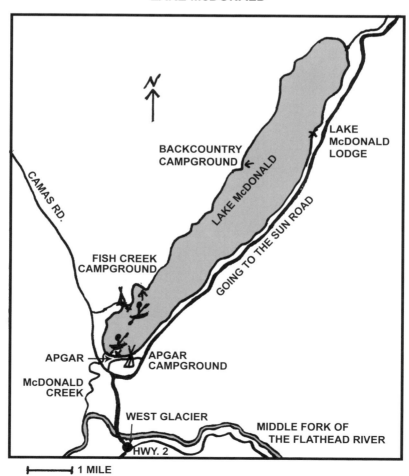

42

the water is always much colder a few inches below the surface – not good if you get dunked!

Directions: Take Hwy. 2 northeast to West Glacier and turn left at the sign to Glacier Park. The park station on this road requires an entrance fee and will provide a park map if requested. Turn left onto Camas Rd. at the first intersection and then turn right approximately ¼ mi. on the Apgar road and proceed to the fishing access (large parking area) on the left after a short curve to the right. To access the Fish Creek Campground, continue 1 mile on Camas Rd. to the Fish Creek Campground Rd. and turn right. Proceed to the picnic area parking for launch beneath the restroom and parking lot.

Photo courtesy of Phyllis Pederson

WOODEN BOAT SKELETON IN LAKE McDONALD

Paddle Notes: Lake McDonald has an iconic beauty with its majestic mountain backdrops, and it's a long lake with plenty of paddling opportunities. Here are two favorites:

1. Apgar to Rocky Point: From the launch, paddle past the dock along the shore to the left (west). You'll pass several Apgar buildings and a motel located at the outflow, McDonald Creek. Pay attention to current here and stay far enough into the lake to avoid being pulled into the creek.

   Numerous old cabins line the lakefront in the Apgar area and are "grandfathered" in terms of private ownership. As you continue paddling towards the northeast along the shore, you'll come to the Fish Creek Campground where you can take out and enjoy picnic tables and public restrooms. Fish Creek flows into the lake at this campground and forms a small gravel delta and surrounding shallows.

Past Fish Creek is a bay where you'll find an old boathouse that used to house

LAKE McDONALD – SOUTH END

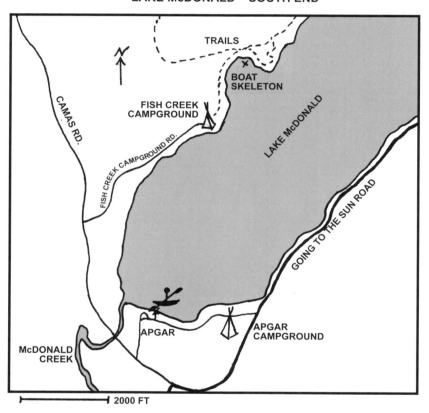

an old wooden park tour boat for Lake McDonald. After the construction of the Going to the Sun Road, the boat was deemed unnecessary (according to park historians) and destroyed. Evidently, it was towed to the middle of the bay and set afire. The bottom hull and one side didn't totally burn and drifted to one side of the bay about 30 ft. from the north shore. Today, if the water is calm and the lighting just right, you can still see the 40 ft. long boat's "skeleton" – (its lower rib planking and one partial side) where it sunk into the shallow (6-10') bottom.

At the northeast end of this bay you'll find Rocky Point and a small, short beach where you can land. True to its' name, there's a rocky cliff area with easily accessible hiking trails. Climbing up near the top of Rocky Point gives excellent views of the lake and provides a great picnic spot. If you continue up the lakeshore past Rocky Point, you will very quickly see the beginning of the burned areas from the 2004 fires.

On the return trip to the launch, you may choose to cross the lake instead of hugging the shore. But, please consider your boat and skill level as strong winds come up within minutes on this lake, often in the afternoon. The middle of Lake McDonald can be deceptively dangerous with choppy waves and icy

LAKE McDONALD, FISH CREEK

cold water, leading to hypothermia in minutes if you capsize.

2. <u>Fish Creek to Backcountry Campground</u>: There's a great beach for launching beneath the parking lot and restroom at the beginning of Fish Creek Campground. Often, there's even shade for loading your kayak if you're planning to camp. (* A backcountry camping permit is required and can be obtained from the ranger station in Apgar.) If you are camping, you should check with the camp ranger/host regarding parking overnight.

From the launch, paddle to the left and past the bay and Rocky Point described in the first paddle. If you haven't seen it, check out the old tour boat skeleton in the bay. Once you pass Rocky Point and start paddling north towards the inflow of the lake, you'll quickly encounter the burned area from the Reynolds Fire. This fire burned near the shoreline for several miles, including the backcountry campground site which is 6-7 miles up the lake.

When you reach your destination, there is a small peninsula and beach on the north side. There are only two campsites, and a pit toilet up the trail past them. There's no enclosure, so it's a "loo with a view!" There are a few unburned trees near the water's edge for shade.

BOWMAN LAKE

Location: 2.3 hrs., 60 mi., N. 48.829 – W. 114.201 (for launch), backcountry campground N.48.904 – W. 114.121
Paddle Craft: Canoe or medium- long sea kayak, no rec. boats
Skill Level: Intermediate
Outing: Approximately 6 mi. to end of lake and backcountry site- 5-6 hrs. round trip, or camping overnight if you have a backcountry park permit.

BOWMAN LAKE

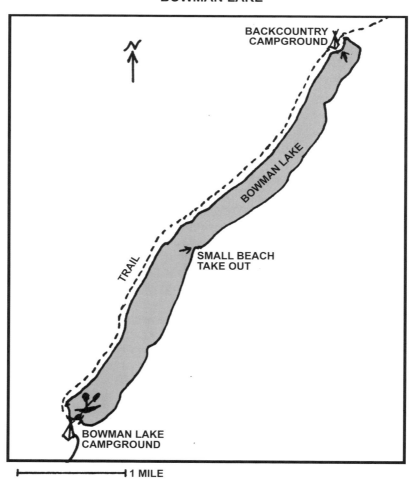

BACKCOUNTRY CAMPGROUND

BOWMAN LAKE

SMALL BEACH TAKE OUT

TRAIL

BOWMAN LAKE CAMPGROUND

1 MILE

Launch Facilities: Beach at campground, campsites, restrooms
Special Interest: Breathtaking views with towering mountains, backcountry campsite (end of lake) - One of the most beautiful lakes in the park, and similar to Kintla.
Caution: The North Fork road is only partially paved, and has a "washboard" surface with potholes for about half the distance. Additionally, from the park entrance, the 6 mile dirt road to the lake climbs and is narrow and winding. High clearance vehicles recommended, and no large campers.
Wind and high waves coupled with a long fetch can be dangerous and make paddling headway impossible, especially in the afternoons. Occasionally, paddlers have to leave boats at the end of the lake/backcountry site and hike back! Remember, this is a cold, high mountain lake, so warm clothing is recommended if you paddle to the end. Also, in May & June, there can be visible clouds of billions of mosquitoes!

BOWMAN LAKE

Directions: Take Hwy. 2 NE to Columbia Falls, and from C. Falls, take the North Fork Road 36 miles to Polebridge. From the historic Polebridge Mercantile (you might want to stop here for yummy pastries and sandwiches), proceed left to the Glacier Park ranger station where park fees apply. From there, it's 6 miles to the Bowman Lake Campground and launch.

Paddle Notes: Scenery here is jaw dropping with the huge glaciated peaks of Glacier Park in the background, coniferous forests at the sides, and icy blue crystal water. From the launch, you can only see a small portion of the lake, and staying close to shore is advisable. For safety reasons, if it's windy, you might want to choose the left (northwest) side of the lake as there's a hiking trail paralleling the lake for its entire length. The trail is rarely adjacent to the lake, however, so a bit of bushwhacking is in order if you're forced off the water.

If the forecast is good and you're lucky, however, you can paddle up the right side of the lake from the launch (or cross over if you're on the left) and pull out half way at a scenic stream gravel bar noted on the map. It's a great lunch and stretch spot with an easy take out (unlike the rest of the rocky shoreline).

The backcountry campsite is on the west side and about a quarter mile short of the end of the lake. You'll find this campsite to be an absolute gem with a rocky stream and log bridge with a handrail separating the sleeping and eating areas. There are 8 small tent sites with an outhouse up the hillside. The trail around the lake is close to the backcountry campsite and continues on to Brown's Pass (about 6-7 miles with a huge climb.) From Brown's pass, you can access Hole in the Wall, a primo backcountry destination, but you should have a backcountry permit (plus your backpack) as it takes all day to get there.

Paddling to the end of the lake from the backcountry campsite is a must for watching wildlife and fishing. Several creeks feed the lake at the end, and the bottom drops off quickly. Because the water is so clear, you can easily see 30-40 ft. below. Large schools of whitefish and occasional trout actively feed at the mouths of these creeks.

If you can get a permit, this is an amazing backcountry camping experience. And, carrying your gear in a kayak or canoe sure beats hiking 7 miles with a backpack!

KINTLA LAKE

Location: 2 hrs., 15 min., 69 mi., Campground: N. 48.935 – W. 114.345, back country campground: N. 48.974 – W. 114.246
Paddle Craft: Sea kayaks, canoes, no rec. boats
Skill Level: Intermediate
Outing: 1-5 hrs. (to end and back) or overnight - backcountry camping (permit)
Launch Facilities: Kintla campground, grassy/gravel launch, restrooms, parking
Special Interest: Spectacular scenery with Kintla Peak and some of the highest peaks in the park, back country campground, very wild and rugged, great wildlife possibilities

KINTLA LAKE

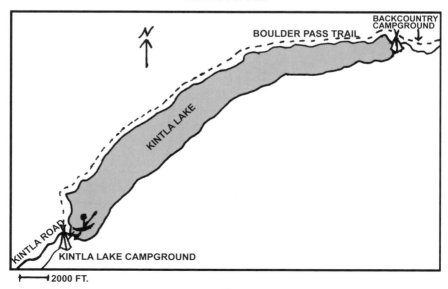

Caution: The road! The North Fork road with washboard and potholes is just getting you warmed up for the 17 miles of dust to Kintla, and at least the North Fork Road is reasonably straight! Needless to say, trailers and low vehicles are NOT recommended. Wind on Kintla, especially in the afternoon, can strand you at the end of the lake just like Bowman. Also, like Bowman, there's a long fetch and the waves can get wicked. Remember, this is a high mountain, very cold lake, so thermal protection is recommended if you're paddling to the end. Also, late spring and early summer can bring visible clouds of mosquitoes!

Photo courtesy of Phyllis Pederson

KINTLA LAKE

Paddle Notes: Kintla and Bowman's scenery just scream "Glacier Park!" And, they're both equally stunning with high mountain peaks as a backdrop for clear, sapphire blue water. If you plan on camping at the backcountry site at the end of the lake, please remember that a park permit is required. (Recommended!)

It's best to start your paddle in the morning when the water is usually calmer. It's about 5-6 miles to the end of the lake and the backcountry campsite, and there aren't any obvious places for a landing and break in terms of a beach. Nonetheless, you can probably find a place to pull over when needed, just don't expect gravel or sand.

It's almost difficult to focus on your paddling on this lake as the scenery is constantly tearing your eyes away. There's a good chance of seeing ospreys, eagles, and maybe moose or bear along the forested shoreline. Areas to take out along the way are few, and there are no good beaches. Once you get to the end, though, the backcountry campsite is an excellent place to have lunch, stretch your legs, and just relax. If you do have a backcountry permit, it's heavenly to set up camp and really enjoy yourself in this remote corner of paradise.

If you're backcountry camping, you might want to consider hiking to Upper Kintla Lake the following day. Or, perhaps tethering your boat and gear and taking your backpack along for further hiking and backcountry camping. This is absolutely amazing, wild country! Be sure to bring bear spray, though.

TWO MEDICINE LAKE

Location: 2 hrs. 10 min., 69 mi., N. 48.484 – W. 113.369, boat dock at the end of the lake is N. 48.474 – W. 113.409.
Paddle Craft: Sea kayak, canoe, SUP for edges of lake
Skill Level: Advanced beginner, intermediate (wind/wave dependent)
Outing: 2-6 hrs. (longer if hiking at end)
Launch Facilities: Gravel beach beside boat launch, parking, restrooms

TWO MEDICINE LAKE

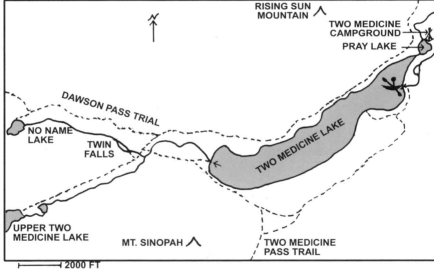

Special Interest: Bring along hiking boots in your boat! Mt. Sinopah, Rising Wolf, other gorgeous mountain scenery plus day hike to Twin Falls and/or Upper Two Medicine Lake at end of lake. Additionally, there is a GNP campground on Pray Lake and a camp store at the parking lot by Two Medicine Lake. Running Eagle Falls is only a mile from the lake (also called Trick Falls because it's a double waterfall) and was named for a famous female Blackfoot warrior in the 1700's. An old wooden tour boat can also take your non-paddling group members to the end of the lake to join you for day hikes (for a small fee.)
Caution: When it gets windy at Two Medicine, it doesn't mess around! It's generally windier on the east side of the park, and if you're camping, unattended and un-staked tents can easily end up blowing away or "tacoed" around trees! Needless to say,

paddling in these conditions is no fun and can be dangerous, so bring a good book! Luckily, it's only like this on occasion. Most of the time, it's breezy or slightly windy, so "skirt the shore" for safety, and wear thermal protection.

Directions: Take Hwy. 2 from Kalispell north to Columbia Falls, and continue on Hwy. 2 around the southern edge of Glacier Park until you reach East Glacier. At East Glacier, take a left under the railroad bridge onto Hwy. 49 and proceed several miles to Two Medicine Rd. where you turn left. Continue to the park entrance (fees apply) and proceed towards the lake. A mile or so before the lake you will see a small parking lot for Running Eagle Falls and it's worth a stop to see this unique double falls with a short handicapped accessible nature trail. Continue to lake where there's a large parking lot and camp store, and take a right for the campground if you're camping.

Paddle Notes: Two Medicine Lake and its campground are not as heavily visited as other parts of Glacier Park because it's not as close to Going to the Sun Road. Prior to the opening of the road in the 30's, however, this area was one of the most heavily visited when tourists arrived by train in E. Glacier and then ventured by horseback to a series of chalets in the park. The Two Medicine Camp store is actually one of the original chalets, although it has been remodeled.

PRAY LAKE & MT. SINOPAH AT TWO MEDICINE

Two Medicine was a spiritual place for native tribes, and continues to be for the Blackfeet. If you're camping and having coffee/tea on the bench beside Pray Lake with Mt Sinopah in front and Rising Sun on the side, it's easy to understand why this place was considered sacred ground and a place for vision quests.

For a short, easy paddle, Pray Lake is accessible from the field adjacent to the campground. In order to access Two Medicine Lake from Pray Lake, however, you'll have to wade and pull your boat up the short stream that connects the lakes.

The best access for Two Medicine Lake is the gravel beach on the east side of the lake at the end of the parking lot with the store. The lake is 2-3 miles long and generally you've got a headwind paddling to the end of the lake. It's a good idea to start in the morning when the lake is calmer. If you stay left as you're paddling, there's a large delta from Aster Creek that's good moose habitat, and you can occasionally spot them swimming in the bay to the left of the launch. Mornings and evenings are the best times to see them.

TWO MEDICINE LAKE LAUNCH AREA

From the tip of the peninsula, it's often a good idea to paddle across to the right side of the lake to minimize waves. You will eventually turn right to access the landing area beside the boat dock at the end of the lake. You can beach your boat to the right of the dock, or even paddle up the stream slightly to a sand/gravel bar.

Hopefully, you've got your hiking boots and a picnic lunch in your boat, as it's really worthwhile to take the half mile hike to Twin Falls, If you have time, continue another mile and a half to Upper Two Medicine Lake (4 mi. round trip.) This is a spectacular high mountain lake with grand vistas and wildflowers along the way. The lake itself is surrounded by high peaks and is in an old cirque that was once the head of a glacier. There's a backcountry camping site here as well (permit required.) It's a bit hard to reach the flat, rocky area across the outflow and logs, but if you can get there, a swim in this lake on a hot summer's day is heavenly! Bring your bear spray, and watch out for moose.

And, by the way, the Two Medicine area is this author's favorite part of Glacier Park! Try it and you'll see why.

ST. MARY'S LAKE

Location: 2 hrs. 40 min, 122 mi., N. 48.691 – W. 113.524
Paddle Craft: Sea kayaks with spray skirts only
Skill Level: High intermediate, absolutely no beginners!
Outing: 4-6 hrs. (if paddling to end of the lake), 1-2 hrs. for Silver Dollar Beach
Launch Facilities: Gravel beach beside boat dock, parking and restrooms
Special Interest: Glacier Park is called the "crown of the continent," and St. Mary's Lake is definitely its crown jewel! This lake is, hands down, the most beautiful lake in the park, in North America, and possibly the world! The majestic pinnacles, glaciated hanging valleys and cirques, colorful rocks, and remnants of glaciers that once carved the peaks invite you to slow down and kick in your childhood sense of wonder. Paddling this slice of heaven is a privilege few get to enjoy because of high winds, so grab this brass ring if you get a chance!

ST. MARY'S LAKE

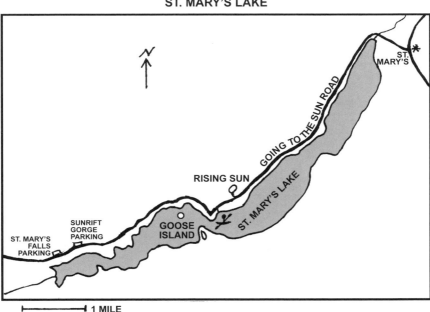

⊢——————⊣ 1 MILE

If time and weather are limited, paddling to Silver Dollar Beach is great short trip from the boat launch. All of the stones are flat here from wind and wave action. Walking barefoot on these smooth, warm stones on a sunny day followed by a swim in the warm water of the lagoon behind the beach is a bucket-list experience!
Caution: The wind! St. Mary's is a dark lady - she's exquisitely beautiful, but can be treacherous and deadly. Gale force winds are fairly common here as katabatic winds often come down from the high peaks in the west. Windsurfers like this lake, but it's even too much for them at times (as well as the park tour boats!) The lake is cold, deep and darkly foreboding, and you know it's windy when you look at some of the trees at the lake's edge - they're bent at 45 degree angles!

There's evidently no way to predict the wind on St. Mary's according to tour boat captains. Afternoons can be calm and mornings wicked, vice-versa, or it can be windy for days. If you get a good forecast and glassy water in the morning, go for it! But, know that conditions can change quickly, so make sure you have good paddling skills, a sea kayak, thermal protection, and a spray skirt.

Directions: Take Hwy. 2 east and north to Columbia Falls, go over the river to the "Y" in Columbia Heights, veer to the left and continue on the same road through Hungry Horse and Coram. At West Glacier, turn left to Glacier Park. After the park entrance (fees apply), continue to the next intersection and take a right onto the Going to the Sun Road. (No vehicles/campers over 21' allowed.) Follow the road over Logan Pass (probably with a few photo stops) and continue past Sunrift Gorge. This area burned last year (2015), but the burn opened up extra views of the lake. Turn right at the boat dock entrance past Sun Point for the launch area. Tour boats leave from this location as well, so if it's too windy to paddle, consider a boat tour (assuming it's not too windy for the tour boats!)

Paddle Notes: St. Mary's is almost "pinched" in half near the boat dock, and by far the most spectacular part of the lake is the west half to the right of the launch. This western section is the paddle described, and is counterclockwise. It's about 6-7 miles to the end of the lake, and the shoreline is irregular and fascinating.

ST. MARY'S LAKE

After launching, you'll paddle along a "wall" of rocks until you reach the opening to the western section where you head right (west). If it's even slightly windy, this area acts as a "pinch point" and funnels the wind and wave energy so that waves are much higher than the rest of the lake. Be aware of this phenomenon before you launch because you have to go through this funnel to reach either the rest of the lake or Silver Dollar Beach. Assuming it's calm and glassy (the author was fortunate to have such a sunny day!), continue toward some of the colorful slab rock walls with small cave indentations on the right. Sunlight creates a "fire on the rocks" phenomenon with dancing reflections that look like gold coins and dancing curtains over the rock faces. Mother nature has also sculpted some perfect rock gardens here with mossy weeping walls, daisies and violets.

An iconic feature you can't miss in the first section of the paddle is Goose Island, probably the most photographed scene in the park. Goose Island is actually two separate, rocky islands (with a few trees) that appear as one island from the shore. They are only separated by a few, shallow feet and you may be able to paddle between them.

ST. MARY'S LAKE – WEST END

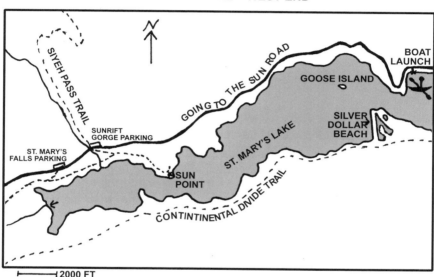

As you paddle, be sure to stop and look up periodically as there's just so much sensory overload on this lake. Photo ops are everywhere! Continuing down the north shoreline, there are numerous small points and coves and several shallow beaches if you need to take out and stretch. As you paddle under Sun Point, you might wave to tourists overhead. And, consider that your kayaks (if you're in a group) add interest to their photos! You'll also notice the large burned areas with mosaics of unburned trees, often near the shore.

As you approach the end of the lake, you should see Virginia Falls which escaped the fire of 2015 unlike its sister, St. Mary's Falls. The beach and delta at the lake's inflow is quite broad and St. Mary's Creek has several meanders between low, flat gravel and muddy areas. Make sure that you find a take out spot with more gravel as it's not fun to sink in the mud. A tiny island with a creek on both sides is a perfect lunch spot.

Heading back on the south side, notice the striking, colorful cliffs. There are two points on the south side that have short beaches where you can take out. And, be sure to notice the huge rock wall with a tree growing up the middle!

SILVER DOLLAR BEACH STONES, ST MARY'S LAKE

When you near the "pinch point," be sure to stop at Silver Dollar Beach, a half mile long peninsula to the right of the channel. All of the rocks here are flat and many look like silver dollars because of wave action from the windy full fetch of the lake. The trees here are also exceptionally crooked, and many are at a 45 degree angles from the wind. It's easy to see that the prevailing wind direction is from the mountains in the west. Be sure to walk barefoot on the warm, smooth stones and swim or wade in the shallow lagoon if weather permits for the ending of a perfect paddle. And, give thanks for the gift of a calm day and paddle on St. Mary's!

MANY GLACIER LAKES

Location: 3 hrs., 148 mi., 1. Northwest primary launch: N. 48.799 – W. 113.663
2. Hotel beach launch: N. 48.797 – W. 113.658
3. Trail take-out, Swiftcurrent Lake: N. 48.789 – W. 113.666
4. Trail at Lake Josephine: N. 48.788 – W. 113.670
Paddle Craft: Sea kayaks recommended for easier portage or boat pull to Lake Josephine, or SUP's if water is calm. Canoes ok, but no rec. boats
Skill Level: Advanced beginner
Outing: 3-5 hrs. for both lakes
Launch Facilities: 1. Northwest end of lake: gravel beach, limited parking, no pit toilet but campground is nearby. 2. Hotel launch: gravel beach, all hotel amenities (but more crowded)
Special Interest: A "two 'fer"! Swiftcurrent Lake & Lake Josephine, two gorgeous high mountain lakes, are both accessible with one paddle. You have a choice of either a ¼ mi. portage on the trail between lakes, or wading & pulling your boat up the creek to Lake Josephine. (Bring a line for your boat for pulling). There's spectacular mountain

scenery, hiking all around lakes and the best area in the park to see grizzly bears on the mountainsides above the lakes.

Caution: Wind/waves- mainly in afternoon, cold water - thermal protection recommended. Many Glacier gets wind, but there's considerably less than St. Mary's Lake or Two Medicine. Also, bring the bear spray for take-outs on these lakes as Many Glacier has one of the highest concentrations of grizzly bears in the park. With that said, bears statistically don't bother groups of 3 or more.

MANY GLACIER LAKES

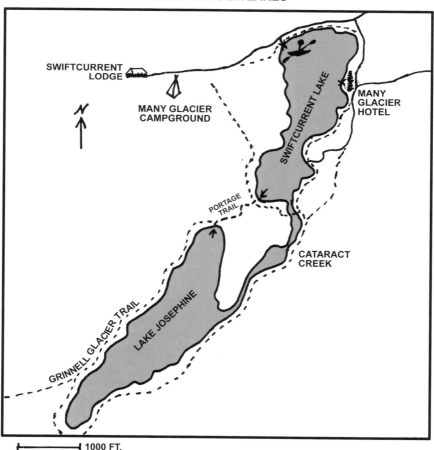

Directions: Take Hwy. 2 east and north to Columbia Falls over the Flathead River, and at the "Y" in Columbia Heights, turn left and continue on the same road. Continue through Hungry Horse and Coram to West Glacier, and turn left to Glacier Park. After the park entrance (fees apply), continue to the next intersection and take a right onto the Going to the Sun Road. (No vehicles/campers over 21' allowed.) Follow the road over Logan Pass (probably with a few photo stops) and continue out of the park to the village of St. Mary's. Turn left on Hwy. 89 and proceed to Babb. Turn left again at the Babb Bar/Supper Club onto Rte. 3 and continue past Lake Sherburne to Swiftcurrent Lake. At the intersection, take a left to the hotel, or continue to the first left after the intersection, a small dirt road that takes you to the Northwest launch area (generally less crowded than the hotel).

Paddle Notes: From the NW launch on Swiftcurrent Lake, it's an easy paddle across to the historic Many Glacier Hotel if you choose, or stop on the way back for ice cream and a cold drink. Paddling south down the west side of the lake gives you the best variety in shoreline, and there are several places to stop for pictures. The glaciated peaks around you with their classic pyramid shapes and snow-capped glacial remnants will grab your attention in any direction. The lower section of the peak to the north of the lake is a good place to scope for grizzly bears with binoculars.

LAKE JOSEPHINE – MANY GLACIER

Both Swiftcurrent Lake and Lake Josephine are relatively small, glacier-fed lakes and are quite cold, even mid-summer. To access Lake Josephine, you have two choices: 1. You can take out at the scenic tour boat dock and portage your boat about a quarter mile on an easy trail (which works best if you're in a group and can help with boat carries.) 2. Wade up the creek (against some current) pulling your boat if the stream is low enough (generally mid-summer to fall.) The rocks at the beginning are a bit tricky around the bridge, but overall it's easier than the portage. And, the scenery is much more rewarding! You may even be able to get back in your boat and paddle at times where it's a little deeper and the current is slower.

Once you're back in your boat, if you paddle on the east side, you'll encounter a small beach a little more than halfway down the lake that's a perfect take out point for lunch. At the south end of Lake Josephine lies Grinnell Glacier and the picturesque cirque that is its headwall. This glacier has receded considerably in recent years as have all the glaciers in the park. Grinnell Glacier carved the valley for both of the lakes you're paddling, and views don't get much better than this!

On the way back, consider riding the easy current down the creek back into Swiftcurrent Lake. And, yes, it will handle sea kayaks – you don't need a whitewater boat. Depending on flow and depth, you might still have to get out and pull your boat some, but you should be fine for most of the way. And, it's a lot more fun and quicker than the portage!

PULLING A BOAT BETWEEN SWIFTCURRENT & JOSEPHINE LAKES, MANY GLACIER

Be sure to check out the Many Glacier Hotel on the way back. It's one of the park's most endearing old hotels with its iconic view of Mt. Wilbur, and it has recently been remodeled and restored. Treat yourself to the huckleberry ice cream as a perfect ending to your day!

NORTHEAST & HUNGRY HORSE RESERVOIR

LAKE FIVE

Location: 45 min., 32 mi., N. 48.462 – W. 114.025
Paddle Craft: Any
Skill Level: Beginner
Outing: 1-2 hrs.
Launch Facilities: Fishing area with paved parking, pit toilet
Special Interest: Glacier Park backdrop scenery
Caution: Wind and waves, mainly afternoons

LAKE FIVE

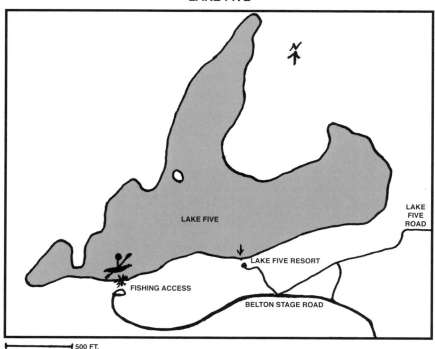

Directions: Take Hwy. 2 north from Kalispell. At the intersection with the Blue Moon bar/ restaurant (past the airport), turn right towards Columbia Falls.
Proceed on Hwy. 2 towards Glacier Park and stay left at the intersection in Columbia Heights. Go past Hungry Horse and Coram, and several miles down the road look for the Lake Five Resort sign. Turn left on Belton Stage Road and stay left for a few miles until you see the sign for Paul's Memorial Fishing Access, and then turn right. (You will pass the entrance to the Lake Five Resort before you get to the fishing access).

Paddle Notes: Lake Five is technically not in the Flathead Valley, but it's close, so it's included in this section. The lake offers easy paddling with the backdrop of mountains in Glacier Park, and it's a relatively peaceful lake in the mornings and evenings, or spring and fall. There are homes on the lake, mostly on the south and east sides, but the lakeshore is not overbuilt.

From the launch, you can paddle a few minutes to the right and pass the Lake Five Resort, an older, established resort with a great beach. The sandy bottom is very clear and inviting for swimming or skills practice, but the resort is private, so stay outside the roped area. During the summer, you might be able to land on either side of the beach and find some refreshments!

From the resort, there are two arms of the lake and the number of homes is slightly less in the upper, northerly arm. As you continue along the north and west shore back towards the launch area, be sure to paddle into the almost hidden cove (looks like a "tail" on the map"). There's a good opportunity to see waterfowl here as well as loons, kingfishers, and herons. Lake Five is a great fall paddle with lots of color along the shore.

ELK ISLAND
(HUNGRY HORSE RESERVOIR)

Location: 2.3 hrs., 50 mi., launch: N 48.267 – W 113.816, Elk Is.: N. 48.241 – W. 113.800
Paddle Craft: Sea kayaks, canoes, some SUP's
Skill Level: Advanced beginner - Intermediate
Outing: 2-3 hrs. over & back (2 mi. to island), or stay overnight.

ELK ISLAND

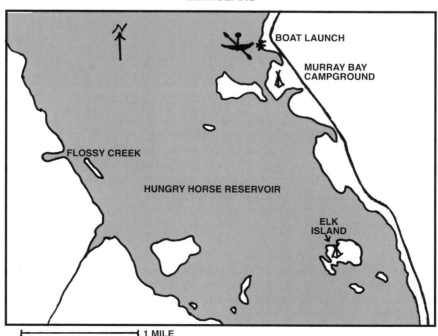

Launch Facilities: "Boat Launch" – rocky area beside concrete launch. Pit toilets available and parking. Also, outhouses on Elk Island & picnic tables.

Special Interest: Island camping, spectacular scenery beneath the "Great Northern" mountain. Also, it's a rare opportunity to paddle a large body of water (30 mi. long) in a wild mountain setting with no residential or commercial development on the entire shoreline. Numerous other islands, bays to explore

Caution: Wind/waves on crossings. Best to camp in spring or fall when it's not crowded because the reservoir is low enough that power boats can't get there

ELK ISLAND CAMPSITE VIEW – HUNGRY HORSE RESERVOIR

Directions: Take Hwy. 2 NE to Columbia Falls, go over the river, and at the "Y", continue through the canyon past Columbia Heights to Hungry Horse. Turn right at the sign for the east side road along Hungry Horse Reservoir. This road goes through the small town of Martin City and does not cross Hungry Horse dam. Once you're a mile down the road, pavement ends and it's a dirt road all the way. Watch for a sign that simply says "boat launch" past mm. 21 and turn right to the launch area which is just north of the Murray Bay campground. This area was recently renovated by the Forest Service (2014) and there may be a fee for parking.

Paddle Notes: To access Elk island, paddle to the left (south) through a narrow channel between the shore and another island right offshore from the boat launch. Once you're through the channel, you'll see Elk Island directly ahead, and it's about 2 miles from the launch. There are numerous other islands in the reservoir, but Elk Island is the only one with established campsites, picnic tables, and outhouse facilities. There's a sign for the campground.

The colorful slopes of the Great Northern Mountain tower above the reservoir on the east and provide a dramatic backdrop for Elk Island. Hungry Horse reservoir varies incredibly in water depth, so the islands and channels change sizes depending on how full the reservoir is kept. Water flow is controlled by the dam and runoff, and during peak runoff, the reservoir can come up as much as a foot per day, so take note to pull boats up sufficiently on the beach.

Mid-June is a good time for camping and catching the peak of the bear grass on Elk Island, and the reservoir is generally too low for camping competition from power boats. Fall is also a great time with the extra color in the foliage against the stunning mountain backdrops. And, mosquitoes aren't generally a problem.

From Elk Island, it's a pleasant morning or afternoon paddle across to other islands and the west shore. Be sure to go up some of the drainages on the east shore where you'll see gorgeous rock formations and the obvious signs of forest fires that have swept through the area. Some of the drainages have short waterfalls as well. Wind often comes up in the afternoon, so be aware that it may take more of an effort getting back.

A campfire on the beach is a perfect way to end the day if you're kayak or canoe camping. The solitude and absence of lights on the shore makes it perfect for stargazing as night arrives.

DEVIL'S CORKSCREW ISLANDS

Location: 2.5 hrs., 63 mi., N 48.109 – W. 113.698, Camping Island: N. 48.110 – W. 113.698
Paddle Craft: Sea kayak or canoe for camping, SUP, others for day trips
Skill Level: Advanced beginner to Intermediate
Outing: 1 hr. - 2 days (for camping), plus 2 day paddles from island - approximately 8-10 mi. round trip each – 3-5 hrs.
Launch Facilities: Beach launch, pit toilet, Devil's Corkscrew campground, limited parking
Special Interest: Remote, wilderness paddling & camping, dark skies for stargazing, no residential or commercial buildings along entire reservoir.
Caution: Wind/waves, especially in afternoon

Directions: Take Hwy. 2 NE to Columbia Falls ,over the river, and at the "Y", continue through the canyon past Columbia Heights to Hungry Horse. Turn right at the sign for the east side road along Hungry Horse Reservoir. This road goes through the small town of Martin City and does not cross Hungry Horse dam. Once you're a mile down the road, pavement ends and it's a dirt road all the way. Continue about ¾ way down the reservoir to the sign for Devil's Corkscrew Campground (approximately 25-30 mi.) and turn right. Launch area is at the campground, which only has room for a few campsites.

Paddle Notes: The camping island (not named) is only a mile from the launch area to the north. Once you're launched, you can see this island to the left of the larger island that's closer. Unless the lake is filled (when there are 2 islands), there's a connecting beach that's a good place to land as well as set up tents. A short trail to the left from the beach goes to another great site for 2-3 tents on the west side of the island, approximately 30' up with a great view. Once you're set up to camp (or if you're day paddling), here's two terrific round trip paddles, approximately 8-10 mi. each:

DEVIL'S CORKSCREW ISLANDS

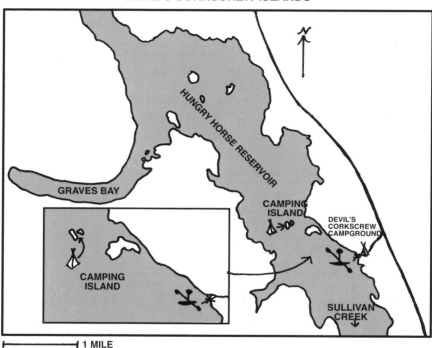

├────────────┤ 1 MILE

- Sullivan Creek- (8 mi. s., not shown on map)- Across and on the west side of the lake, there are two creek areas to the south that are worth checking out. The first indentation on the map is Forest Creek, and this creek is fairly small, but the bay is nice. Further south (and, unfortunately, off the map) is Sullivan Creek, which extends quite a ways west. There are high canyon walls here and often you can see fish around the bridge. It's a gorgeous, pristine bay.

- Graves Bay & Islands- Paddling north of the camping island, you'll find that the reservoir opens up to a large bay with three islands in the middle that are worth exploring. Then, head slightly southwest into Graves Bay, a long open channel with scenic islands at the mouth. This is a great place to watch for bears and other wildlife. Round trip to the end of Graves Bay is about 10 miles.

WESTERN LAKES

ASHLEY LAKE

Location: 50 min., 30 miles, N. 48.213 – W. 114.617
Paddle Craft: Any
Skill Level: Beginner
Outing: 1-3 hrs.
Launch Facilities: Fishing access with grassy launch area, pit toilet, parking (Also possible to launch at the N. Ashley Lake campground)
Special Interest: Medium sized lake with gorgeous emerald and aqua colored bays, loons are common.
Caution: Winds and boat traffic mid-summer

Directions: There are two ways to get to Ashley Lake:
1. Head west out of Kalispell on Hwy. 2, and turn right onto Batavia Lane. Proceed for several miles to the "Y" with Sherman Road, and stay straight as the road becomes S. Ashley Lake Road. Continue west towards the lake and turn right (slightly before lake) onto NF 912, N. Ashley Lake Road. Continue to the fishing access and turn left (sign).
2. Head west out of Kalispell on Hwy. 2 past Kila and Rogers Lake Road. Look for Ashley Lake sign and turn right onto S. Ashley Lake Road. Follow this road

ASHLEY LAKE

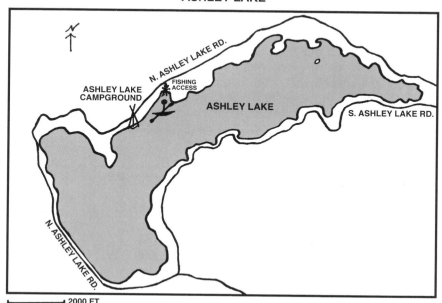

to the south part of the lake and turn left onto N. Ashley Lake Road (NF 912). Proceed past Ashley Lake North campground to fishing access and turn right (sign) to launch.

Paddle Notes: Ashley Lake has a number of shallow, sandy bottom areas that make the beautiful aqua-emerald green color along the shoreline and in a few center sections of the lake. And, the rolling hills and towering pines, spruce, and larch provide a verdant backdrop for the lake. Houses along the lakeshore are numerous and range from small cabins to large homes, and most are located on the northeast shore of the lake. So, the paddle described goes from the launch counter-clockwise into the southwestern section of the lake. Fall and spring are the best seasons for serene paddling and listening to loons.

Following the shore to the right of the launch, you will pass the North Ashley Lake Campground. You may want to check it out on the way back (and, it's another possible launch spot). Continue around the point to the right of the campground where there's a bay surrounded by National Forest land. This is a shallow, grassy/reedy area that provides a quiet home to waterfowl and possibly a few turtles. There are no houses in this northwestern bay.

Proceed south along the shoreline and watch and listen for loons, as they are very common on this lake (except during heavy boat traffic). You will pass a few homes as you paddle south, but the area is generally quite peaceful. At the south end, there's another large and shallow marshy bay. There is a public dam here with a small spot to take out and stretch if you wish. There's also a small island you may be able to paddle around, but this area is a mud flat, so channels may not be open. Ospreys and eagles can often be seen fishing here.

As you start paddling north up the west side of the lake, there are several homes along the way. Once you reach the section of the lake that curves to the right (east), continue straight and you will encounter another large shallow area with a small island (depending on lake water level). The bottom is sandy here, so the water has a range of aqua colors. This is an excellent place to swim or practice skills where you might get wet. From here, it's easy to cross the lake back to the point near the campground and make your way back to the launch. The campground on the way is small, but you might want to check it out.

LITTLE BITTERROOT LAKE

Location: 33 min., 24 mi., Blue Grouse Park- N. 48.136 – W. 114.736, second small launch area near Bitterroot Lions Youth camp – N. 48.639 – W. 114.714
Paddle Craft: Any
Skill Level: Beginner
Outing: 1-2 hrs.
Launch Facilities: Blue Grouse Park- picnic area (2 tables), boat launch, limited parking, pit toilet. Small launch area- gravel beach only, 1-2 cars max.
Special Interest: Small island surrounded by marshes at north end of lake- great waterfowl habitat

Caution: Possible wind/waves, boat traffic (more in southern section of lake) as lake has many cabins/homes

Directions: Take Hwy. 2 west from Kalispell towards Marion. At the top of the Marion

LITTLE BITTERROOT LAKE

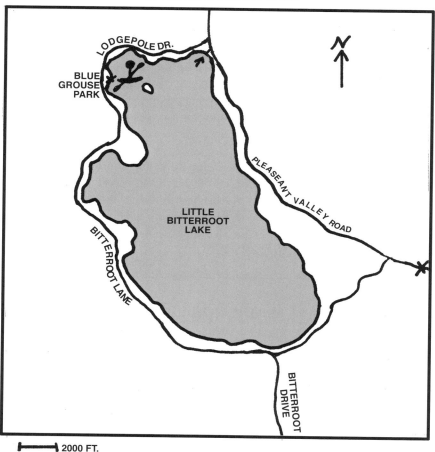

LITTLE BITTERROOT LAKE

2000 FT.

hill, turn right onto Pleasant Valley Rd. Between the gas station and restaurant. Proceed about 2.5 miles to a "Y" in the road. Bitterroot Drive will be on the left. You can go either way, but it's a bit shorter to stay on Pleasant Valley Drive to either launch area. Continue past the Bitterroot Lions Youth Camp and immediately after the camp on the left you'll see a small pull off that's a possible launch area. However, there is only room for 1-2 vehicles (and no facilities.) If you choose to go to the main launch area at Blue Grouse Park, continue to the intersection with Lodgepole Dr. and turn left. It's a little over a mile to Blue Grouse Park, so watch your odometer and turn left at a small dirt road that opens up into the park. This is a small park, but there is room for several vehicles.

Paddle Notes: Bitterroot Lake has quite a number of houses and cabins, but the northern section of the lake is less populated with a more interesting shoreline. There's also less wind and boat traffic because this part of the lake is shallower and better suited to paddling. So, it's a more pleasant outing and the north section was paddled in a clockwise direction.

From the launch, paddle left around a pretty shoreline, especially in the fall with golds and reds from the Tamaracks and brush. Most of the homes are small, quaint cabins, so they add some charm to the landscape. As you continue east to the Bitterroot Lions Youth Camp, you'll pass the other launch area along the way. From the camp, proceed south along the shore as far as you're interested in going. Or, for a shorter paddle, cross back to the island.

The island has shallow marshes that extend from the shore all around it. This is excellent bird habitat, and it's fun to paddle through the reeds. You can generally do this without getting stuck. If you want to land on the island, though, just be aware that going through the reeds all the way to the shore can be difficult, and be careful to avoid stepping into the muck! From the island, it's a short paddle back to the launch, or go down the west shoreline for more exploring.

McGREGOR LAKE

Location: 40 min., 32 mi., N. 48.042 – W. 114.867
Paddle Craft: Any
Skill Level: Beginner
Outing: 2-3 hrs.
Launch Facilities: Gravel beach and boat launch, parking, pit toilet

McGREGOR LAKE

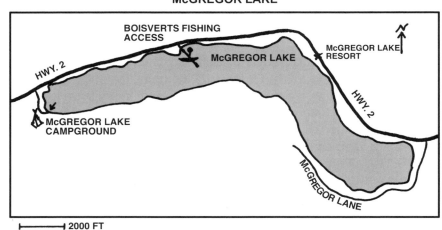

Special Interest: Easy, scenic paddle with golden Tamaracks in the fall, forested south shore of western section of lake with less boat traffic - also McGregor Lake Lodge for meals/snacks after the paddle
Caution: Wind/waves

Directions: Take Hwy. 2 west from Kalispell past Marion to McGregor Lake. The launch is at the Boisverts fishing area after mm. 88 and off the highway to the left.

LAKE McGREGOR WITH LIFTING FOG

Paddle Notes: McGregor Lake is a large, popular fishing lake with houses/cabins around several sections of the lake. The southeast side of the lake has deeper water and therefore usually has more boat activity. The western part of the lake has fewer houses and thus is a quieter, more scenic area to paddle. This is especially true in the fall with golden Tamaracks and misty water. Often, if you start out in fog around 9:30-10a.m. (usually late September & October), it lifts around 11a.m., and if you're on the water at that time, it's a magical thing!

Paddling the western section counterclockwise, head to the right from the launch past some of the houses and cabins. There are two sets of cabins/houses along the north shore, and then the edge of the lake is simply forested. If the water is glassy, you'll see some large rocks on the shallow bottom that are fun to paddle over.

At the western end of the lake (about a mile) is Lake McGregor campground, and it's a convenient place to pull out for a break if needed. At the beginning of the south section of the lake, there's a small boat launch that could also double as a kayak launch if you don't wish to start at Boisverts.

Paddling along the south shore of this western section is quiet and peaceful, and there are no cabins. As you continue heading east, you'll eventually want to cross back over to conclude the paddle, unless you decide to venture into the other end of the lake or circumnavigate.

If you're hungry or thirsty when you get back, consider stopping at the McGregor Lake Lodge. There's a restaurant and bar with a back deck and picnic tables overlooking the lake. And, they make an absolutely amazing Reuben sandwich!

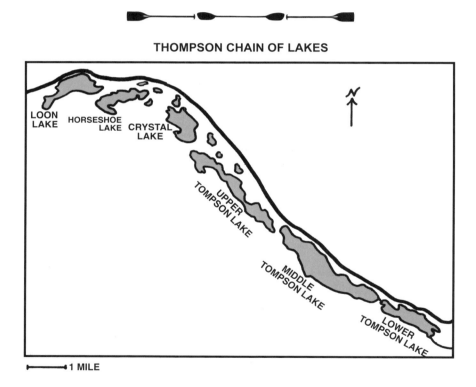

THOMPSON CHAIN OF LAKES

MIDDLE & LOWER THOMPSON LAKES

Location: 50 min.-1hr., 46 mi., N. 48.04 – W. 115.10
Paddle Craft: Any
Skill Level: Beginner
Outing: 1-4 hrs., 2-4 mi.
Launch Facilities: Small unmarked/no name camping area beside Middle Thompson Lake, pit toilet, edge of lake launch.

Special Interest: Paddling through reed/cattail "trails"
Caution: None

Directions: Take Hwy. 2 west past Marion and McGregor Lake, and look for mm. 79. There is no sign at the launch/camping area, but it's right after you pass Lower Thompson Lake. You'll also see a steep dirt hillside on the right across from the camping area and a concrete public outhouse and open gate at the unnamed campground. This launch site is at the lower end of Middle Thompson Lake. Logan State Park is another launch site further up the lake.

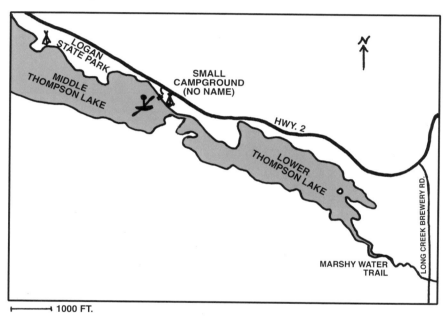

Paddle Notes: The ideal time to paddle the Thompson Lakes is in the fall. Often on late September or early October days, there will be fog in the morning that gradually lifts around 10-11a.m. to reveal glorious sunshine with all the accompanying fall colors. If you're launching as the fog lifts, it's a magical and almost surreal experience.

The most interesting paddle is to the left and through the outflow and reeds into Lower Thompson Lake. There's a wide water trail through the cattails and reeds that winds around for a little less than a quarter mile and takes you to the upper section of Lower Thompson lake. This meandering channel is quite shallow and sometimes you can spot fish swimming below.

Once you enter the lower lake, you'll paddle by a concrete boat launch and a campground. Occasionally in October, you can find spawning salmon here as this is the only section of the lake with a rocky bottom. The shoreline of this lake is varied and pleasant, and as you continue paddling towards the lower end of the lake, you'll see a tiny island to the left that's a great place for a picnic.

From the island, it's a short distance to the outflow of the lake that looks like it's protected by impenetrable reeds. If you look closely, though, you'll find a narrow path that you can just barely paddle through. You'll have to keep your paddle high, and it's

LOWER THOMPSON LAKE REEDS WATER TRAIL

slow going in this section, but it's only about a hundred yards before it opens up to much easier paddling. Water lilies and cattails are abundant here, and you can paddle this winding course in fairly open water for at least another half mile. The turn around point is a culvert that forms an impasse. Power boats and even fishing boats don't come into these channels because of the shallow water, so it's a fun adventure!

HORSESHOE LAKE

Location: 1 hr., 51 mi., N. 48.083 – W. 115.169
Paddle Craft: Any
Skill Level: Beginner
Outing: 1-1.5 hrs.
Launch Facilities: Gravel shore and boat launch at north shore camping area, pit toilet, picnic area, and limited parking
Special Interest: Gorgeous little jewel of a lake with clear, aqua/turquoise water and two delightful islands (one of which has large trees shading a nice beach), camping along north side of lake. Also, warm water for swimming mid-summer as lake is relatively shallow
Caution: Rough road, low vehicles not recommended, and campsites are taken early during mid-summer and weekends.
Directions: Take Hwy. 2 west past Marion, McGregor Lake, and the Thompson Lakes. After you pass Happy's Inn and mm. 72 (at .7 mi. past Happy's Inn), turn left

on Horseshoe Lake Rd. (dirt road). At both the first and second "Y," stay right. This road is bumpy with some sizable potholes. There is camping all along the north shore, and the launch is near the middle of this area. It's almost a mile from the beginning of Horseshoe Lake Rd. to the launch.

Paddle Notes: Circumnavigation of this little lake is only about 2.5 - 3 miles, but the shoreline has lots of interesting nooks and crannies, and there are two lovely islands to add to the lake's charm. It's the aquamarine to emerald green, crystal clear water that catches your attention here.

HORSESHOE LAKE

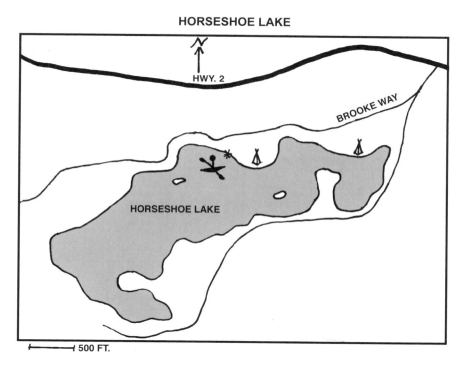

Slightly to the right from the launch is the first island with mature trees and a beach that provides a great place for kids to play or for a picnic. Proceeding counterclockwise around the lake, you'll enjoy the northwest shore where the camping ceases and it's simply forested. There's an almost hidden cove that dips to the southeast with shallow aqua water. The sandy bottom is clear here, and it's great for swimming, plus it's a secluded place to paddle.

Continuing east, the second island appears as the lake narrows to open again at the final bay on the east side. Again, the lake is shallow here with a relatively clear bottom. Paddling back along the northeast shore you will notice most of the lake's camping areas. The lake and camping spots are located away from Hwy. 2, so there's very little road noise to disturb a leisurely paddle and campout.

LAKE KOOCANUSA – SOUTH DAM AREA

Location: 2 hrs., 81 mi., N. 48.414 – W. 115.317 (launch), N. 48.461 – W. 115.296 for northern tip of Yarnell Island.
Paddle Craft: Sea kayak or canoe recommended
Skill Level: Advanced beginner - Intermediate
Outing: 2-4 hrs. for day paddle, overnight for camping
Launch Facilities: Gravel beach, parking, restrooms at recreation area
Special Interest. Lake Koocanusa was created as a joint recreation, flood protection, hydroelectric power, and reservoir project between the U.S. and Canada with the construction of Libby Dam on the Kootenai River in 1972.
The name is a combination of the Kootenai River, Canada, and the U.S.A. This huge reservoir is 48 miles long from the dam to the Canadian border.

There's camping on rocky, tree-covered islands (or singular island if the reservoir is low and exposes the connection.) with picnic tables and several camping spots. Additionally, the reservoir shoreline is irregular and interesting, and it's possible to have lunch/snacks at Koocanusa Resort & Marina.
Caution: Wind/waves, cold water early in season

Directions: Take Hwy. 2 W. from Kalispell to Libby, MT (approximately 1.5 hrs). From Libby, head north on California Ave. (Hwy. 37) along the Kootenai River as the road heads back east. After several miles, take a left on Big Bend Road which comes into NF 228 (National Forest Dev. Rd). and proceed towards the Libby Dam. Immediately after the dam, take a right on Souse Gulch Rd. to the parking lot for the launch. The Souse Gulch Recreation Area is just north of the launch, and it's considered safe to leave locked vehicles overnight if you're camping.

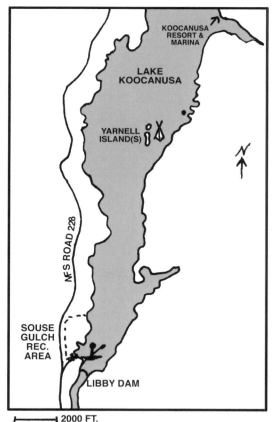

LAKE KOOCANUSA – SOUTH DAM AREA

KOOCANUSA RESORT & MARINA

LAKE KOOCANUSA

YARNELL ISLAND(S)

NFS ROAD 228

SOUSE GULCH REC. AREA

LIBBY DAM

N

2000 FT.

Paddle Notes: It's 3-4 miles to Yarnell Island, the camping destination. Paddle north from the launch along the western, rocky shoreline of the Souse Gulch Recreation area. After the point, you'll see a large, roped-off swimming area that's located in a small bay. If it's a hot day, you might consider a swim, or keep it in mind for your trip back.

From the swimming area, cross over the reservoir to the east side where there's a large, interesting bay to explore. A small creek comes into the reservoir here, and it's good bird habitat in the shallow bogs.

As you paddle north along the east shore, the reservoir opens up and you will soon see Yarnell Island(s). The majority of the time there are two islands, but if the reservoir is low, they're connected and considered one. Most of the camping and landing areas are on the west side of the island(s), so stay on the east side of the reservoir as you're paddling north. Or, when you get there you can easily circumnavigate and pick your landing and camping spot. There may be power boaters camping here as well, although there's better access for kayaks and canoes. There's a nice, shallow beach and a large, flat open field (somewhat rocky) at the northern tip of the island with a picnic table in the trees. This area makes a great camping spot for a small group.

If you're camping for two nights, it's suggested that you explore the reservoir to the north the next day. In particular, take a credit card or cash with you for lunch at the Koocanusa Resort & Marina located in a bay approximately one mile north of Yarnell Island. You might also consider swimming here, so remember to take your suit. There's a landing beach on the north shore near the resort. If you're eating lunch, the picnic tables have some great lake views!

There are no other marinas, businesses, and very few homes on this section of the reservoir and that makes it a serene, natural setting for a paddle. And, the reservoir is so large that boat traffic is generally not an issue.

Enjoying an evening campfire and stargazing is a must for campers. However, there's not much wood on the island, so you might want to bring your own or pick up some driftwood along the shore in the bays along the way.

NORTHWESTERN LAKES

UPPER STILLWATER LAKE

Location: 1+ hr., 43 mi., N. 48.60 – W. 114.66
Paddle Craft: Any (and consider pulling a whitewater boat)
Skill Level: Beginner (except for whitewater option)
Outing: 2-4 hrs., 3-7 miles
Launch Facilities: Campground and pit toilet, boat launch, river inflow
Special Interest: Old historic mill site, possible short whitewater ride, portage and remote, serene paddle on outflow river in upper flat water section.
* Note: You can pull a whitewater boat if you want to run the short cascades and rapid at the old mill site. Spring is the best season for this option and this lake.
Possible backcountry camping, no permit required

UPPER STILLWATER LAKE

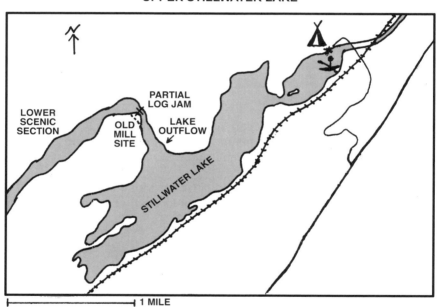

Caution: Two short rapids beside old mill site- ONLY for whitewater boats (short turning radius, "pinch point", and wave trains can easily overturn recreational & sea kayaks, canoes, or SUP's.) Additionally, water is very low late summer & fall

Directions: Take Hwy. 93 to Whitefish and turn left towards Eureka (still Hwy.93) at 2nd street intersection in Whitefish. You'll pass Lower Stillwater Lake and the Stillwater Bar about 10+ miles west on the left. Keep going past mm.151 and turn left at the sign to Upper Stillwater Lake. Continue on the dirt road to the lake and camping area. This road can be rough and muddy. You'll cross the railroad tracks and a bridge over the river that flows into the lake. The river inflow is at the launch site.

Paddle Notes: After launching, paddle over the shallow end of the lake where there's lots of aquatic vegetation and a large beaver home. After paddling over the shallows, a narrow channel to the left will take you to the rest of the lake where the water gradually gets deeper.

Once you enter the main body of water, stay slightly to the right and you'll eventually come to a long channel that leads to the outflow of the lake. Large rocks and slab formations form part of the lake bottom in this area and the water is crystal clear. On hot sunny days, it's a good place to swim as the current is negligible in this first section.

The channel ends at a partial old log dam that's now compromised and is currently a spillway with a series of cascades and small rapids. As you get closer to the log jam, the current becomes noticeable, so look for the rock slab takeout to the left. Caution: You don't want to get caught in the cascading rapids unless you're in a whitewater boat!

After landing the boats, you can easily drag them up on the flat rocks and grass. This site once housed an old homestead and a small mill, and if you explore a bit, you'll see the remains of an old cabin and some outbuildings. The rock formations beside the cascading river offer a perfect picnic location. Camping is totally primitive here and all your gear would need to be carried in your boat. There is an old logging road extending away from the old mill area, but it likely runs through private land.

If you're up for further exploring and paddling, you'll find a trail at the edge of the woods for a short portage. You'll first have to maneuver your boat (hopefully with a partner) down the step like sections of the rock formations. Then you carry it about 150 yds. to the lake-like section of the Stillwater River right below the final small rapid.

This lower section extends for a couple of miles before you notice current and are stopped by a quick drop with even faster current. This should be your turn around point because the current gets faster until the river flows through a rocky canyon with class 3-4 rapids - not recommended for sea kayaks or canoes! If you put in the effort to portage and paddle this section, you'll be rewarded with a serene and beautiful wild area with no signs of civilization other than hearing an occasional train in the distance. Cliff swallows, ospreys, or eagles may even circle overhead as you paddle

DICKEY LAKE

Location: 1hr., 52 mi., North Campground: N. 48.719 – W. 114.832 South Campground: N. 48.708 – W. 114.813
Paddle Craft: Any
Skill Level: Beginner
Outing: 1-2 hrs.
Launch Facilities: Boat launch/swimming area, gravel beach, parking and pit toilets at North Campground – similar at South.

Special Interest: Two campgrounds with incredibly clear, aquamarine water, great swimming and skills practice, light boat traffic even in mid-summer.
Caution: Wind/waves in stormy conditions
Directions: Take Hwy. 93 to Whitefish, turn left to continue on 93 towards Eureka.

DICKEY LAKE

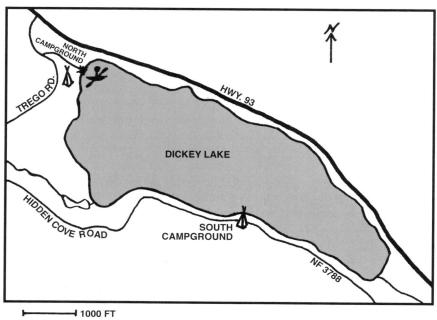

Both entrance roads to the lake are past the community of Stryker. The main launch is the North Campground, and you will see a sign for Dickey Lake as you pass it. Turn left at Trego Rd. and then take the first left at the sign for the North Campground. It's a quarter mile to the launch area.

If you choose to launch at the South Campground, you will turn left onto NF (national forest) road 3788 about a mile before you reach the lake. Follow this road to the campground, and note that after the campground it turns into Hidden Cove Road that joins into Trego Road, so you can loop back to Hwy. 93.

Paddle Notes: It's about 3 miles to circumnavigate the lake and the paddle described is counter-clockwise. After launching, paddle south (to the right) towards the marshy inflow of the lake where you'll find plenty of cattails. You'll notice the incredibly clear aqua water and light, sandy bottom for a good deal of the lake until you get to the marsh. Watch for kingfishers, red-winged blackbirds, and an occasional blue heron.

Continue paddling to the east towards the South campground. There's another swimming beach here and a small side take-out. It's a good place for lunch, or lounging in the sun in a grassy opening up from the lake. There are also two picnic tables in the shade.

As you head to the outflow end of the lake on the southeast side, there are other greenish to aqua sections of the lake that are good places to swim or practice paddling skills. Dickey Lake is a great destination for a hot summer's day as there's less boat traffic than lakes closer to towns. Sometimes it's worth the drive!

LAKE KOOCANUSA – NORTH BORDER AREA

Location: 1.5 hrs., 78 mi., launch: N. 48.960 – W. 115.152, Gateway Campground: N. 48.997 – W. 115.166
Paddle Craft: Sea kayak or canoes recommended, no rec. boats
Skill Level: Advanced beginner-low intermediate
Outing: Day trip 4-5 hrs., or overnight camping
Launch Facilities: Gravel beach, parking, no pit toilet or water
Special Interest: Lake Koocanusa was created as a joint recreation, flood protection, hydroelectric power, and reservoir project between the U.S. and Canada with the construction of Libby Dam on the Kootenai River in 1972.
The name is a combination of the Kootenai River, Canada and the U.S.A. This huge reservoir is 48 miles from the dam to the Canadian border.
Kayak camping is highly recommended at Gateway campground. This campground

LAKE KOOCANUSA – NORTH BORDER AREA

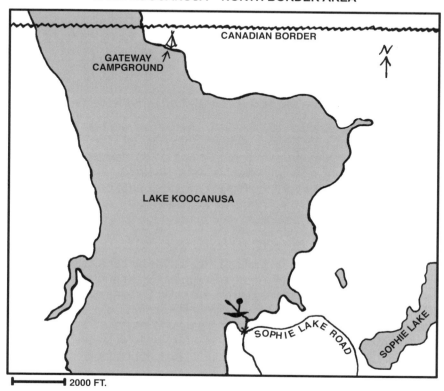

gets very little usage because of limited access (no roads) and boasts a beautiful, peaceful setting with Ponderosa pines and open areas, an outhouse, picnic tables and a driftwood beach facing the sunset. It's also interesting to paddle to the border to see the marker and line of cut trees that delineates the border for its entire length.

Caution: It's okay to paddle into Canadian waters, but DO NOT LAND on Canadian shoreline as there are border patrol boats, cameras, and security measures that could cause you problems, even with a passport. Other cautions are wind, waves and cold water - thermal protection advised in spring, early summer. Additionally, when the reservoir level is very low, it may be a long haul uphill from your boat landing to your camping site for carrying gear.

GATEWAY CAMPGROUND BEACH – LAKE KOOCANUSA NORTH BORDER

Directions: Take Hwy. 93 north to Whitefish. Then, head west on 93 to Eureka, and approximately 1.5 miles past Eureka, turn left onto Hwy. 37. Proceed 1-2 miles west towards Rexford until the road veers south. At that point, stay on the Old State Hwy. 37 for ¼ mile. Then turn right onto Sophie Lake Road and stay on this road past both Tetrault and Sophie lakes. Approximately two miles past Sophie Lake (the road is heading west at this point), turn right onto 7303 (gravel road) and proceed less than ¼ mile to the launch area. It is considered safe to leave locked vehicles overnight if you are camping.

Paddle Notes: It's approximately 3 miles to the Gateway campground, and you can paddle straight across or do slightly more mileage along the shoreline. This makes for a safer and more interesting paddle as there are several coves and bays to check out. The scenery is mostly open country without many signs of civilization. Also, there's very little boat traffic (even mid-summer) as it's a good distance from populated areas on either side of the border. The lake is over a mile wide at places and there will be plenty of privacy along the shore. Eagles and ospreys are common overhead.

If you like driftwood, there are several beaches where you can stop along the way. But, there's plenty of driftwood at Gateway, so there's no need to gather firewood on the way.

Once you get to Gateway, the landing site is a combination of rocks, logs, and gravel. There are no designated camping sites, so find your perfect spot and enjoy the view, which is splendid at sunset! It's also fun to walk the long beach looking for unusual driftwood. As daylight fades, a campfire on the beach is a great way to end your day. As an extra treat, there's very little light pollution, so the stars and Milky Way on an inky black night are mesmerizing!

If you paddle to the border, you'll find a fence and an obelisk delineating the border site. In addition, notice the line of cut trees on each side that runs the entire length of the border between the two countries. Again, please remember not to land on Canadian soil and provoke possible hassles.

GATEWAY CAMPGROUND – SHORE VIEW

SWAN VALLEY

SWAN RIVER TO SWAN LAKE

Location: 45 min., 40 mi., Porcupine Bridge: N. 47.887 – W. 113.861, take out: N. 47.935 – W. 113.854

Paddle Craft: Any, but shorter sea kayak or canoe recommended

Skill Level: Advanced beginner

Outing: 2-3 hrs. plus shuttle time

Launch Facilities: Riverbank only (with a short climb down), limited parking, no restrooms

Special Interest: Serene, winding river that flows through a wildlife refuge, great bird watching, old homestead near middle of the outing

Caution: Late summer, fall trip only! The river and debris (trees) have to "settle out" as the flow slows down. Otherwise, this stretch can be dangerous with logs and branches that can sweep you out of a boat or trap you. This is an "easy river" ONLY later in the year. Also, wind/waves as you cross the lake from the mouth to the take-out can be an issue, especially in the afternoon. Check the forecast before launching as smaller boats, SUP's may have trouble crossing.

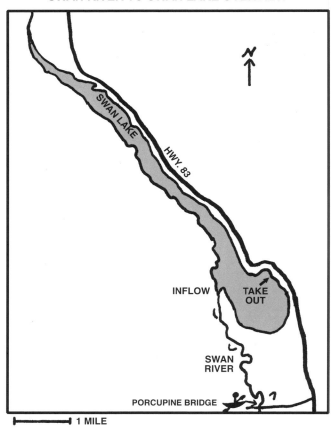

SWAN RIVER TO SWAN LAKE OVERVIEW

Directions: Take Hwy. 93 south toward Somers and at the light, take a left onto Hwy. 82. At the next intersection with Hwy. 35, take a short right and then left onto the Swan highway (83) at the intersection near the Little Brown Church. Continue southeast, and in a few miles, Swan Lake will be along the highway on the right. Note the take out (boat launch) after the large curve to the left near the end of the lake and leave a vehicle for the shuttle as this is a one way trip. After you pass the south end of the lake, look for Porcupine Road (NF 10229) and turn right. Follow this gravel road to the Porcupine Bridge and park off the road on either side of the bridge.

82

Paddle Notes: Depending on river flow, look for the easiest access to the river. Generally it's on the west side, but low flow could make a nice sandbar on the east. The first mile of this trip has the most log-jams, so don't be surprised if the river banks look like "pick up sticks." But, they won't be a problem If your timing (late summer, fall) and the flow is right as all of the debris will have settled out to one side or the other. The river is at least 20' wide or wider in most places, and paddling against slow current is not a problem.

This section of the river in late summer and early fall is generally calm and incredibly scenic as it winds through the Swan River National Wildlife Refuge. Moose are commonly seen feeding or swimming here, so pay attention when you paddle around a bend. Beavers, bears, deer, and coyotes also make their homes in this lush habitat. Binoculars are an asset here as the bird watching is fabulous. And, maybe an eagle or osprey will swoop down in front of your boat for a fish!

SWAN RIVER TO SWAN LAKE

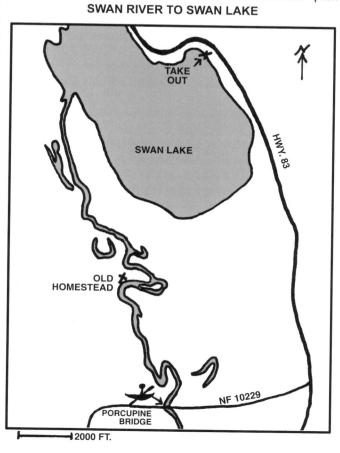

There are several side channels, oxbows, and sloughs along the way to the lake. Approximately half way to the lake in one of these meandering areas, you'll see a quaint old homestead cabin that's fun to explore. Just be careful of loose and rotting boards, nails, and other hazards.

There are numerous places along this winding river where you'll find sand and gravel bars to take out for a rest, picnic, or just to stretch your legs. As you approach the opening to the lake, there's a long bar to the right and some reeds where herons like to hang out. Once you're out of the river mouth, head for the point directly across the lake because the landing site is near the bay behind the point. Your crossing may be windy with some good waves in the afternoon. So, stay together for safety as you cross. And, if you're with a group, but not shuttling vehicles, there are picnic tables and a restroom while you wait for friends to return.

HOLLAND LAKE

Location: 1 hr., 10 min., 72 mi., N. 47.441 – W. 113.616
Paddle Craft: Any
Skill Level: Beginner
Outing: 1-3 hrs.
Launch Facilities: Dirt beach near group camping area, pit toilet at group site, several parking spots
Special Interest: Paddling across lake and hiking to spectacular Holland Falls
Caution: Sudden storms with high wind/waves, boat traffic mid-summer

Directions: Take Hwy. 93 south toward Somers and at the light, take a left onto Hwy. 82. At the next intersection with Hwy. 35, take a short right and then left onto the Swan highway (83) at the intersection near the Little Brown Church. Continue southeast past Condon and watch for the sign for Holland Lake (mm.35-36.) Turn left and follow the road to the sign for the group campsite. The launch is right past a road that turns to the right and goes over a bridge at the outflow (SW end) of the lake.

HOLLAND LAKE

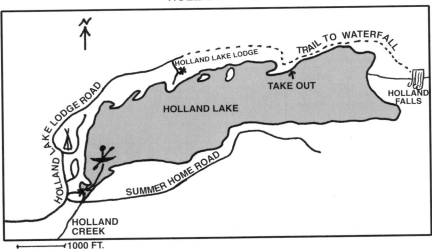

Paddle Notes: After a few paddle strokes from the launch, the lake opens up past the reeds and there's a slight current to paddle against as you're on the lake's outflow. The opening soon widens and suddenly you get a breathtaking view of the lake! Holland Lake is nestled beneath the highest, most jagged peaks of the Swan mountains. And, as you paddle further, you'll see Holland Falls which looks like a bridal veil cascading down the lower mountainside at the end of the lake. With the falls, this lake is likely the most scenic in the Swan Valley.

You'll paddle by the swimming and camping areas on the north (left) side of the lake and a grassy peninsula that's part of Holland Lake Lodge. The peninsula juts out into the lake past the campground, and it's ok to land there if you want to check out the lodge or get some refreshments from the restaurant.

84

Continue paddling on the north side of the lake as it has a more convoluted shoreline with several small bays and two islands. Past the islands, there's a short bay and a point, and once you pass this point, start looking for the take out near a small creek outflow with a tiny gravel beach. The creek's hidden in some brush, so look closely. After landing, you'll need to pull boats/boards up into the bushes. Start climbing upwards and you'll soon meet a narrow trail that connects to the main hiking trail to Holland Falls. (Don't make the mistake of paddling clear to the east end to try and join the trail. Access is nearly impossible there because it's very steep and brushy.)

Another way to get to the falls is to start hiking from the end of the road near the lodge, but you can access the trail much quicker from the lake as you cut half or more of the distance with paddling. And, it's more fun!

The hiking trail is gravel and rock, and hiking boots/shoes are recommended as it's at least a mile to the falls. Along the way, you'll climb to some stunning vistas

HOLLAND FALLS

of the entire lake, the Mission Mountains, and snowfields. Once you get to the rocky outcrop near the falls, the chipmunks and ground squirrels will welcome you. Hopefully, you've brought a lunch or snack so you can sit back on the rocks and enjoy the view and cool spray from the falls.

If you choose to paddle back on the south side of the lake, you'll pass a brushy delta from the waterfall and some rustic cabins along the way. And, if you're hungry or thirsty, check out the Holland Lake Lodge restaurant. The home-made apple pie is terrific!

LINDBERGH LAKE

Location: 1hr., 25 min., 78 mi., N. 47.404 – W. 113.725
Paddle Craft: Any, but longer boats preferable for paddling to end of lake
Skill Level: Beginner to advanced beginner
Outing: 2-4 hrs.
Launch Facilities: Grassy beach, pit toilet, parking, and camping area
Special Interest: Beautiful, long, fairly isolated lake with few houses/cabins, superb mountain views between the Missions and Swan mountains, possible hike from the end of the lake to Crystal Lake (approximately 3 mi. round trip.)

Lindbergh Lake was named for Charles Lindbergh (it was originally called Elbow Lake) when he came to MT and visited the lake following his historic solo trans-Atlantic flight. Supposedly, he carved "Lindy," his nickname, on a rock at the north end of the lake. It could be just a story, but fun to check out!
Caution: Winds from the south or southwest can produce waves that make it tough to paddle.

Directions: Take Hwy. 93 south toward Somers and at the light, take a left onto Hwy. 82. At the next intersection with Hwy. 35, take a short right and then left onto the Swan highway (83) at the intersection near the Little Brown Church. Continue southeast past Condon and past the sign for Holland Lake. About 1.5-2 mi. past the Holland Lake Rd., turn right onto the Lindbergh Lake Rd (71). Proceed approximately 3 mi. to Meadow Lake Rd. (possible sign for campground) and turn right. From there, it's less than a mile to the campground and launch at the north end of the lake.

Paddle Notes: The lake is about 4 mi. long and if you plan to paddle to the end and hike to Crystal Lake and back, make sure you have enough daylight. The mountain views on either side make this lake an exceptionally nice paddle, especially in the fall when the hillsides are a golden mosaic of tamaracks (larch).

Paddle to the right from the launch and head around the point as there are no houses/cabins on this side of the lake. As you paddle south along the western shore of the lake, there are a few sections of cliffs, especially at the northern end. There are also a few bays with gravel beaches, one of which is a small delta from an intermittent creek. This area makes a great lunch stop. There's an osprey nest about a half-mile down from the gravel beach, so check out any fledglings that might still be in the nest. This side of the Mission mountains is wilderness, so it's possible to spot bear, elk, or moose along the way.

With so many mountains around, the wind on Lindbergh Lake is fickle, and it can change directions several times during your paddle. Generally, you get a southwesterly tail-wind in the afternoon for a nice ride back, but don't count on it.

LINDBERGH LAKE

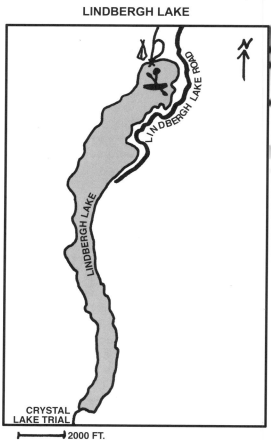

CRYSTAL LAKE TRIAL
2000 FT.

The end of the lake is boggy at the inflow, but there's a spot to land slightly to the right (and before the end of the lake) where you can take out for the trail to Crystal Lake. Or, just stretch your legs and have a snack! Kingfishers and Great Blue Herons are frequent visitors, as well as loons.

LINDBERGH LAKE WITH GOLDEN TAMARACKS (LARCH)

On the way back, paddle on the opposite side of the lake for a slightly different experience. There are houses and cabins on this side, but only on the northeast end. After your return, if you're camping, you might enjoy a swim, campfire, and perhaps some stargazing as evening sets in. Just be sure you're not here in May or June, or the mosquitoes will chase you to your tent!

LAKE ALVA

Location: 1.5 hrs., 80 mi., N. 47.306 – W. 113.576
Paddle Craft: Any
Skill Level: Beginner
Outing: 1-1.5 hrs.
Launch Facilities: Small Gravel beach, pit toilets, NFS campground area and limited parking (Another place to launch is due north almost to the end of the lake. There's a great beach and swimming area near a boat launch).
Special Interest: Easily accessible lakeside campground for a pretty little lake with turquoise edges, the Swan and Mission mountains on either side – campsites are spread out so you hardly see camping neighbors. Some sites are designed mainly for tents.
Caution: Afternoon storms and wind/waves

Directions: Take Hwy. 93 south toward Somers and at the light, take a left onto Hwy. 82. At the next intersection with Hwy. 35, take a short right and then left onto the Swan highway (83) at the intersection near the Little Brown Church. Continue southeast past Condon, Holland, and Lindbergh Lakes. Hwy 83 goes right beside Lake Alva, so watch for the turn onto the campground road at the south end of the lake where you'll find the launch and a turn around with parking.

Paddle Notes: Lake Alva is a pristine, forested little lake with a long, spread out camping area on the east side, and no houses along the lakeshore. It's the total opposite of the Lake Inez directly south which is surrounded by homes and does not appear to have public access. Lake Alva is a paddling gem in comparison.

To the left of the launch (going counterclockwise), there's a stretch of aqua colored water shortly before the outflow of the lake. There isn't much current, so it's hardly noticeable. Continuing north along the heavily forested meandering western shore, there's an island around midway with a small area on the south side where you can land. Or, a bit further up there's another aquamarine bay with a point and small beach.

The northern marshy part of the lake is good bird and moose habitat. As you head back south on the east side, there's a boat launch and a really nice beach that's adjacent to a roped off swimming area. So, if it's a warm summer day, enjoy the clear water and superb scenery before you head back to the launch. And, it's a great place to practice your wet water skills.

LAKE ALVA

BOAT LAUNCH
SWIMMING AREA

HWY. 83

LAKE
ALVA

LAKE
ALVA
C.G.
ROAD

OUTFLOW

1000 FT.

CLEARWATER CANOE TRAIL

Location: 1.5 hrs., 89 mi., Seeley lake launch: N. 47.213 – W. 113.521, Canoe Trail parking take-out (or launch): N. 47.226 – W. 113.536
Paddle Craft: Any (shorter boats recommended or SUP's)
Skill Level: Beginner
Outing: 2-3.5 hrs. (includes shuttle time, or return)
Launch Facilities: Lake launch: small sand/gravel beach, parking, but no restrooms, Canoe Trail parking lot (take-out or launch): pit toilet, grassy launch
Special Interest: Slow, winding water trail with great potential for wildlife and birds, also diverse aquatic vegetation and turtles. Trail can be paddled upstream and back with launch from north shore, or one way with shuttle.

Caution: Water flow for Clearwater River – best as a mid-summer paddle as flow can be too fast with debris in spring, and too low in the fall.

Directions: Take Hwy. 93 south toward Somers and at the light, take a left onto Hwy. 82. At the next intersection with Hwy. 35, take a short right and then left onto the Swan highway (83) at the intersection near the Little Brown Church. Continue southeast past Condon and Lakes Alva and Inez.

CLEARWATER CANOE TRAIL OVERVIEW

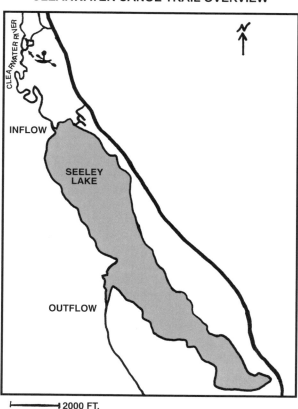

If you are shuttling or launching from Canoe Trail parking lot, proceed as follows: Approximately 2 miles before Seeley Lake, go past the Boy Scout Road and then turn right on Elaine's Way. Continue a short distance past buildings as the road veers to the left. Watch for a dirt road on the right and proceed to the Canoe Trail parking lot.

If you are simply paddling upstream and back, continue past Elaine's Way and MT Fish Wildlife and Parks offices a few miles north of Seeley Lake. Turn right onto a paved road with commercial buildings and a parking lot at the northeast section of Seeley Lake. The launch is a short dirt road off these roads (see map).

Paddle Notes: Seeley Lake is a large, popular lake in the summer with a significant amount of boat traffic due to its many resorts and cabins. The Canoe Trail is a terrific paddling alternative when the Clearwater River current slows down in the summer. It's easy to paddle upstream because there's not much current, and not many folks think of enjoying this beautiful stretch going in both directions.

The small beach near Rice Creek (an intermittent stream) is the launch and has a few reeds in front of it before the open water. Paddle across the north end of the lake and head for the mouth of the river behind the point. If it's mid-summer, there are plenty of water lilies along the way. There's some current at the mouth, but it should still be easy going. The river varies in width, but is usually wide enough for 2-3 boats.

It's both relaxing and fun to meander around the many curves in the river and anticipate

CLEARWATER CANOE TRAIL

what you'll see around the next bend. The water is exceptionally clear (hence the name, Clearwater) and there's lush aquatic vegetation on the banks and bottoms of this winding waterway. Some of the aquatic plants actually have underwater flowers in whites and pinks, so enjoy the show. Turtles are abundant on many of the logs, and it's great fish habitat as well. Watch for footprints on the banks where deer, moose, bear, and possibly elk come down to drink. There are usually kingfishers around and possibly herons, osprey, eagles, and songbirds.

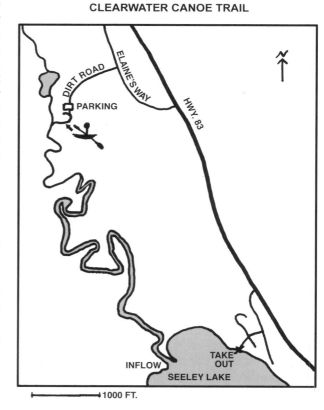

CLEARWATER CANOE TRAIL

As you paddle near the parking area, the channel narrows and you should see a turn to the right that's part of an old oxbow. It's a short distance to the landing where you can take out and stretch your legs, find the pit toilet at the north end, and have a picnic. Or, shuttle back if that was your plan. Paddling back, especially in early evening, is especially rewarding with a little boost from the current.

PLACID LAKE

Location: 1.hr., 45 min., 99 mi., North end – N. 47.133 – W. 113.523, Placid Lake campground, southeast end – N. 47.118 – W. 113.503
Paddle Craft: Any (for shoreline), sea kayaks, canoes for crossings
Skill Level: Beginner - Advanced beginner
Outing: 1.5-3 hrs.
Launch Facilities: 1. North end: Small section of Placid Lake State Park that's on the northeast shore - limited parking, pit toilet, launch near dock at trough.
Special Interest: Water lilies in summer, wetlands that provide excellent bird and wildlife habitat on north and western shores. Possible shuttle with two launch spots.
Caution: Wind/waves for crossings, boat traffic and wave runners

Directions: Take Hwy. 93 south toward Somers and at the light, take a left onto Hwy. 82. At the next intersection with Hwy. 35, take a short right and then left onto the Swan highway (83) at the intersection near the Little Brown Church. Continue southeast all the way past Seeley Lake for several miles. Then, turn right onto Placid Creek Rd and head west about 3 miles.

PLACID LAKE

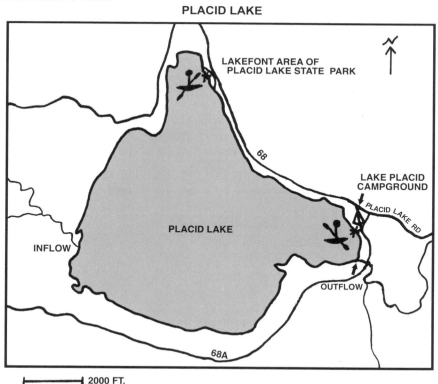

To access the north launch area, turn left on S. Placid Lake Rd. (68A) when you come to an intersection, and then a quick right onto 68, N. Placid Lake Rd. Continue 2-3 miles towards the north end of the lake where there is a small section of Placid Lake State Park on the water. Look for a small opening on the left near the end of the lake, and launch by the dock.

To access the campground launch, simply turn left at Road 68, N. Placid Lake Rd., and proceed to the gravel beach, dock area.

Paddle Notes: The paddle described is from the north launch. It's easier here to access the north and west sides of the lake where you'll find fewer homes and more wildlife habitat. The southeast campground launch is an easier group launch site, however, and has a gravel beach and more room for vehicles. You can also leave a car there for shuttle if you plan on paddling 2/3 of the way around the lake.

Ponderosa pines make a nice backdrop for the launch. If this lake is paddled in mid-summer, there are a number of water lilies and cattails as you enter the water as well as subsurface vegetation with small flowers. You can paddle across the north end of the lake, but the extensive marshes prevent access to the end of the lake. This is a great place to see Great Blue Herons, ospreys, and kingfishers, as well as turtles lounging on logs.

Paddling south along the shore, you will come to a point with a bay that joins the west shore. After the point, the houses taper off because there's no road access. Again, you'll find marshes as you continue down the west side to the lake's inflow. There's not much current, so it's interesting to paddle up the outflow for a bit. It's possible to see moose, bear, beavers, and river otters on Placid lake, and they're more likely to be on the west side. There are plenty of waterfowl too, so it's nice to have binoculars with you.

From this point, you can circumnavigate the lake (5-6 mi.), paddle to the campground launch and end your paddle there (if you've left a vehicle for shuttle), or simply go back to the north launch. And, you will have avoided much of the boat traffic in the middle of the lake.

SALMON LAKE

Location: 1 hr., 45 min., 100 mi., South end: N. 47.086 – W. 113.394, North end: N. 47.109 – W. 113.429
Paddle Craft: Any
Skill Level: Beginner
Outing: 1.5-3 hrs., each end
Launch Facilities: 1. South end: Gravel beach beside boat dock at campground, restrooms and parking 2. North end: Pull off from Hwy. 83, slight hill and launch area below with boat carry, no restrooms/pit toilet
Special Interest: Salmon Lake is one of several natural lakes in the Clearwater River chain that includes Seeley Lake. It's a popular boating location with wonderful paddling opportunities at each end of the lake. 1. South end: Water lilies in summer, excellent state campground along lakeshore, easy paddle with picturesque cabins and rolling hills, forest. 2. North end: Water trail through reeds and marshes, lots of waterfowl, charming evening paddle

Caution: Boat traffic, mostly in middle areas of the lake, afternoon winds

Directions: Take Hwy. 93 south toward Somers and at the light, take a left onto Hwy. 82. At the next intersection with Hwy. 35, take a short right and then left onto the Swan highway (83) at the intersection near the Little Brown Church. Continue southeast past Condon and Seeley Lake to Salmon Lake State Park, approximately 8 miles south of Seeley Lake.

Paddle Notes: The most appealing sections of Salmon Lake for padding are at the north and south ends, and there's less boat traffic in these locations.

South end: Heading south (left) from the launch at the campground, paddle around the point to a small bay filled with water lilies in the summer. It's easy to paddle amongst the lilies, and dragonflies may charm you by landing on your boat.

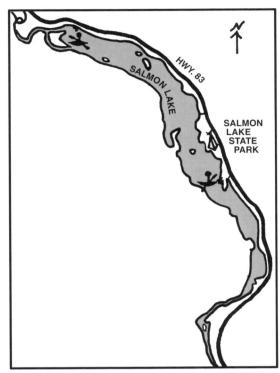

SALMON LAKE OVERVIEW

2000 FT.

WATER LILIES ON SALMON LAKE (SOUTH END)

From the point, cross over to the west side where the shoreline is more diverse. There are numerous cabins and two church camps on this south section of the lake, but they're far enough apart to blend in nicely with the towering Ponderosas, Western Larch, and Douglas Fir.

Continuing south on the west side, there's a large peninsula that acts as a "pinch point" for the lake, and the peninsula houses the largest of the church camps with many outbuildings. The next section of the lake is open before it pinches again, and there's a wetland on the east side that's a good place to spot grebes, songbirds, and waterfowl. The common loon can also be found here during the summer when boat traffic is light.

As the lake narrows past this last open area, there are a number of rocks and boulders in the channel, and some current as this is the beginning of the lake's outflow. The current here is easy to paddle against, so you might want to continue downstream for awhile. The river here is wide enough for a few boats and scenic with an occasional rustic cabin and opportunity to see beavers, mink, and possibly moose.

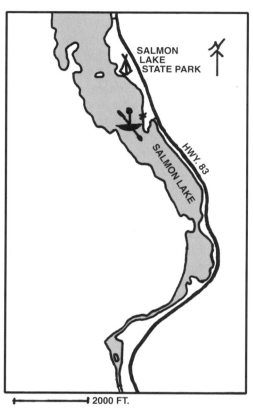

SALMON LAKE – SOUTH END

NORTH SALMON LAKE WATER TRAIL

If you continue south, there's one more small opening with an island and another rocky section where the river narrows and current increases. From this point, you may want to turn back as paddling gets difficult.

North End: This end of the lake is highly recommended for an early morning or evening paddle with golden light (evening) and the opportunity to see more birds and wildlife (beavers like these channels!) From the launch, you'll paddle to the right to find the water channel with brush along the shore. It's actually wide enough for a few boats and the current is easy to paddle against.

SALMON LAKE – NORTH END

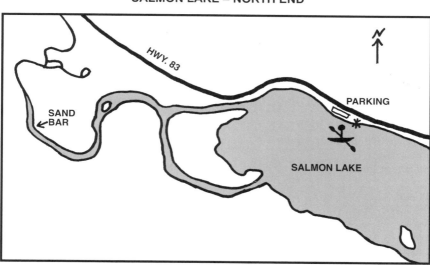

You'll quickly come to the intersection for the outflow and the bottom of the "C." Paddle right, and as you round a bend, there's a tiny island. Going further, you'll encounter a small sand/gravel beach that's wide enough for a few boats to take out. This is a perfect snack or dinner spot to watch the occasional heron, eagle, or waterfowl. It's possible to go further up, but the channel narrows and starts "braiding" making the route confusing. Coming back, take the channel to the right for the south section of the "C," and check out the island down and across from the launch for more wildlife before you head back.

COMPILATIONS, RECOMMENDATIONS

*These compilations follow the chapter's site order.

BEST SITES FOR QUICK PADDLES AND BEGINNERS

- Foy's Lake
- Church Slough
- Creston Jessup Mill Pond
- Somers Bay
- Wayfarer's Park
- Lake Five

BEST SITES FOR CAMPING (DRIVE-TO) & KAYAK CAMPING

Campgrounds
Whitefish Lake
Tally Lake
Lake Mary Ronan
Wayfarer's Park
Other campgrounds on Flathead Lake
All of the lakes in Glacier Nat. Park
Ashley Lake
McGregor Lake
Middle & Lower Thompson Lakes
Horseshoe Lake
Upper Stillwater Lake
Dickey Lake
Holland Lake
Lindbergh Lake
Lake Alva
Placid Lake
Salmon Lake

Kayak Camping
Lake McDonald Backcountry site
* Bowman Lake
* Kintla Lake
Elk Island
Devil's Corkscrew Islands
Lake Koocanusa – S. Dam area
Lake Koocanusa – N. Border area
Upper Stillwater Lake

* Not in spring, early summer
  because of mosquitoes

SEASONAL SITE LIMITATIONS

Smith Lake – spring, early summer only, water too low late summer, fall
Somers Bay & Wayfarer's Park – summer, fall (lake is too low in spring)
Bowman Lake & Kintla Lake – mid-summer, fall (too many mosquitoes early)
Hungry Horse Reservoir – reservoir is "full pool" mid-summer, so sites often taken
Upper Stillwater Lake – Not enough water for good paddling late summer, fall
Swan River to Swan Lake – late summer, fall only, too much flow early is dangerous
Clearwater Canoe Trail – summer best because of easy flow

AUTHOR'S RECOMMENDATIONS

Somers Bay – utterly charming and best evening, quick, and beginner's paddle
Smith Lake – best bird watching paddle in spring, early summer
Echo, Peterson, & Abbott Lakes – good spring paddle with shoreline interest
Lake McDonald (GNP) – most accessible park lake, outstanding anytime
Two Medicine Lake (GNP) – favorite camping/paddling place in park, least crowded
Elk Island – favorite kayak camping spot, late spring or early summer
Middle & Lower Thompson Lakes – favorite fall paddle late morning when fog lifts
Upper Stillwater Lake – favorite spring, early summer paddle

ACKNOWLEDGMENTS

For the past five years since I first published a short booklet with a similar title (and only 12 locations), I've had a lot of encouragement from paddling buddies and retailers to get a "real book" completed. Researching, compiling, completing, and editing a book is a huge project. And, like all of life's big endeavors, it's almost never a solo effort. It takes a team, so I've got a lot of folks to thank.

First, I'd like to thank my spouse and paddling partner, Jon Maxwell, for his support, encouragement, and taking care of "stuff" while I was glued to my chair and computer for the many hours this book demanded. And, getting this book published wouldn't have been possible without the assistance and encouragement of my editor friends, Jean Kramer, Anne Clark, and Eddie Greene. Jean acted as my primary editor, and endured some late nights, bleary eyes, and sacrifice of personal time to help. She was amazing in finding the typos, missing words, and redundant adjectives that I kept using. Anne Clark had helped me format the original paddling booklet, and provided great feedback and final editing on this book as did Eddie Greene on the beginning sections. I'd also like to acknowledge and profusely thank my brother, Jim Pederson, for his time, creativity, and help with the maps for the first booklet and wizardry with photos for this edition.

Of course, putting this book together wasn't all work. The paddling part was a lot of fun! I've been blessed to be a member of the local Flathead Paddlers group for 14 years. My paddling buddies from this group enthusiastically shared ideas for paddling sites, and accompanied me on the outings or campouts to check them out. So, thanks to everyone in the Flathead Paddlers group for all the support and great times! I'm afraid that if I start listing all the folks who paddled with me over the years as I made location notes, I might miss someone, so thanks to everyone in the group. You know who you are!

A few special thanks to those who specifically suggested sites, accompanied me on research paddles for notes, or both: David Bixby and Linda Bailey for the Swan Valley; Anne Clark for Lake Five and McGregor Lake; Scout Crawford for Lake Mary Ronan, Devil's Corkscrew Islands, and Lake Koocanusa – south dam area; and Benita Noble for Horseshoe Lake.

I also need to acknowledge all the folks who make "Google Maps" possible, 'cause I used it a lot! This tool was invaluable not only for maps, but for confirmation of directions to sites and paddle notes. It's just so cool to be able to zoom down on a spot as a reminder!

A special inspirational thanks goes to my friend, Susan Conrad, who just published "INSIDE, One Woman's Journey Through the Inside Passage" (May, 2016). Her solo sea kayaking journey from Anacortes, WA to Juneau, AK in 2010 gave her heroine status in my mind, and her commitment to publishing her book (which I highly recommend!) was a constant reminder for me to work on this one.

Thank you all, and happy paddling!

Debbie Arnold

GO FORTH AND PADDLE!
~Debra J. Arnold~

FLATHEAD LAKE NEAR PAINTED ROCKS

ABOUT THE AUTHOR

After paddling a canoe for 20 years, Debra (Debbie) Arnold slipped into a friend's kayak, paddled for the first time on alternating sides of the boat, and felt a huge smile creep across her face! Within weeks, she had visited every kayak shop within 150 miles, read everything she could get her hands on, demoed a dozen boats, and finally purchased her first kayak and a lightweight paddle (The first paddle she tried felt like it weighed 10 pounds).

Then, it was on to instruction to gain confidence in this new passion. She had learned through cross country skiing that form and function are inseparable and that practicing good form in any sport leads to efficiency, ease of movement, and a lot more fun. So, learning good paddling form became an obsession.

Over the years, Debbie has taken over 250 hours of professional instruction, much of it from attendance for 9 years at the Pacific Sea Kayak Symposium in Port Townsend, WA. Here she received instruction from some of the top kayakers in the world, including two Olympians who taught forward stroke classes (her favorite). Other classes dealt with equipment, navigation, safety, and trip planning. Additionally, she has completed advanced skills courses from the University of Sea Kayaking and SKILS, a Canadian professional kayaking instruction group that teaches the military.

With a professional background as a safety consultant, Debbie has an abiding interest in paddling safety, and in teaching others to be safe on the water. From her experience as a science teacher (physics in particular), she also has an interest in boat design, and how the form (design) of boats affects their function (movement in the water, ease of paddling, and re-entry). She has personally demoed over 200 boats (mostly kayaks, but several canoes and SUP's) to see how they perform (and, of course, to find her favorites)!

Debbie considers her main kayaking credentials to be the many miles she has put on boat and blade. She lives in Kalispell in the beautiful Flathead Valley of Northwestern Montana, a place considered to be a slice of paddling heaven where she's paddled for 17 years. She also loves the ocean and has paddled extensively on the Pacific coast of Vancouver Island, the Gulf Islands, and the San Juan Islands in Washington.

Many of these trips have been group kayak camping adventures and mini-expeditions for up to 10 days (Hot Springs Cove and The Broken Islands, B.C.). She has been blessed to paddle with great friends, humpback whales, dolphins, seals and sea lions, millions of starfish and anemones, and to camp from her kayak on gorgeous wild surf beaches with fresh wolf prints. But, she continually finds new kayaking adventures close to home with a seemingly endless supply of pristine water to paddle and explore in Montana.